Secret Smithsonian Adventures

CLAWS AND EFFECT

SUPER
AWESOME

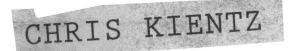

CHRIS KIENTZ

STEVE HOCKENSMITH

LEE NIELSEN

SMITHSONIAN BOOKS
WASHINGTON, DC

Secret Smithsonian Adventures

CLAWS AND EFFECT

SUPER AWESOME

Story by
Steve Hockensmith and Chris Kientz

Illustration by
Lee Nielsen

Color by
Lee Nielsen

Assistant Colorist
Keil Hunka

Lettering by
Dalaney LaGrange

Original Research by
Anthony Bellotti

This book may be purchased for educational, business, or sales promotional use.
For information, please write: Special Markets Department,
Smithsonian Books, P.O. Box 37012, MRC 513, Washington, DC 20013

Published by Smithsonian Books
Director: Carolyn Gleason
Production Editor: Christina Wiginton

Library of Congress Cataloging-in-Publication Data is available upon request.
Manufactured in the United States of America
20 19 18 17 16   5 4 3 2 1

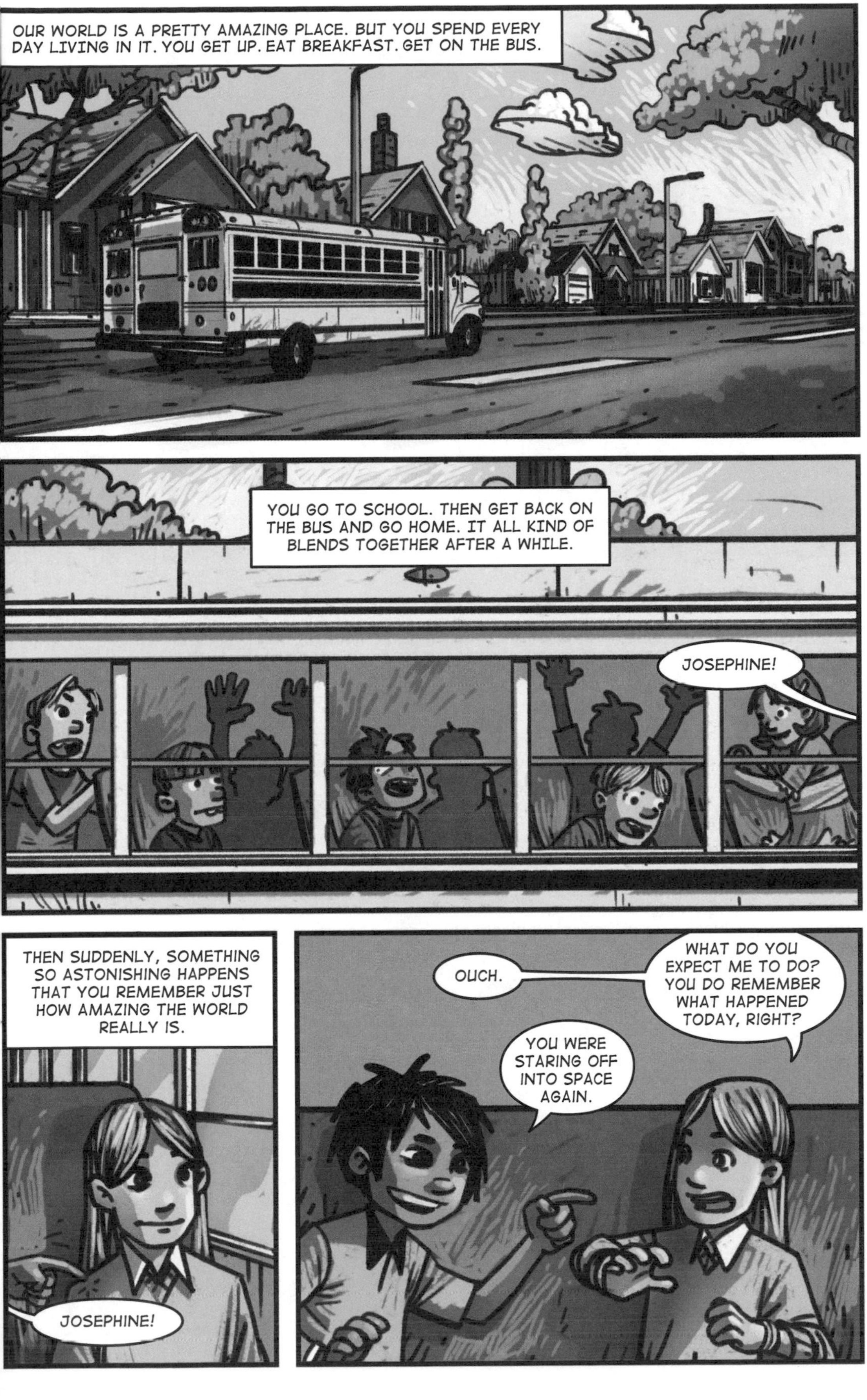
OUR WORLD IS A PRETTY AMAZING PLACE. BUT YOU SPEND EVERY DAY LIVING IN IT. YOU GET UP. EAT BREAKFAST. GET ON THE BUS.
YOU GO TO SCHOOL. THEN GET BACK ON THE BUS AND GO HOME. IT ALL KIND OF BLENDS TOGETHER AFTER A WHILE.
JOSEPHINE!
THEN SUDDENLY, SOMETHING SO ASTONISHING HAPPENS THAT YOU REMEMBER JUST HOW AMAZING THE WORLD REALLY IS.
JOSEPHINE!
OUCH.
WHAT DO YOU EXPECT ME TO DO? YOU DO REMEMBER WHAT HAPPENED TODAY, RIGHT?
YOU WERE STARING OFF INTO SPACE AGAIN.

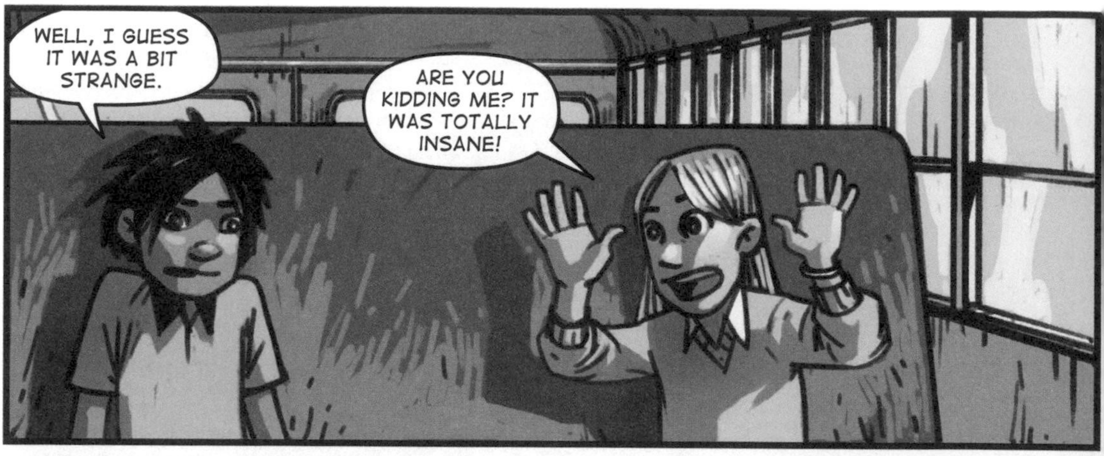
WELL, I GUESS IT WAS A BIT STRANGE.
ARE YOU KIDDING ME? IT WAS TOTALLY INSANE!

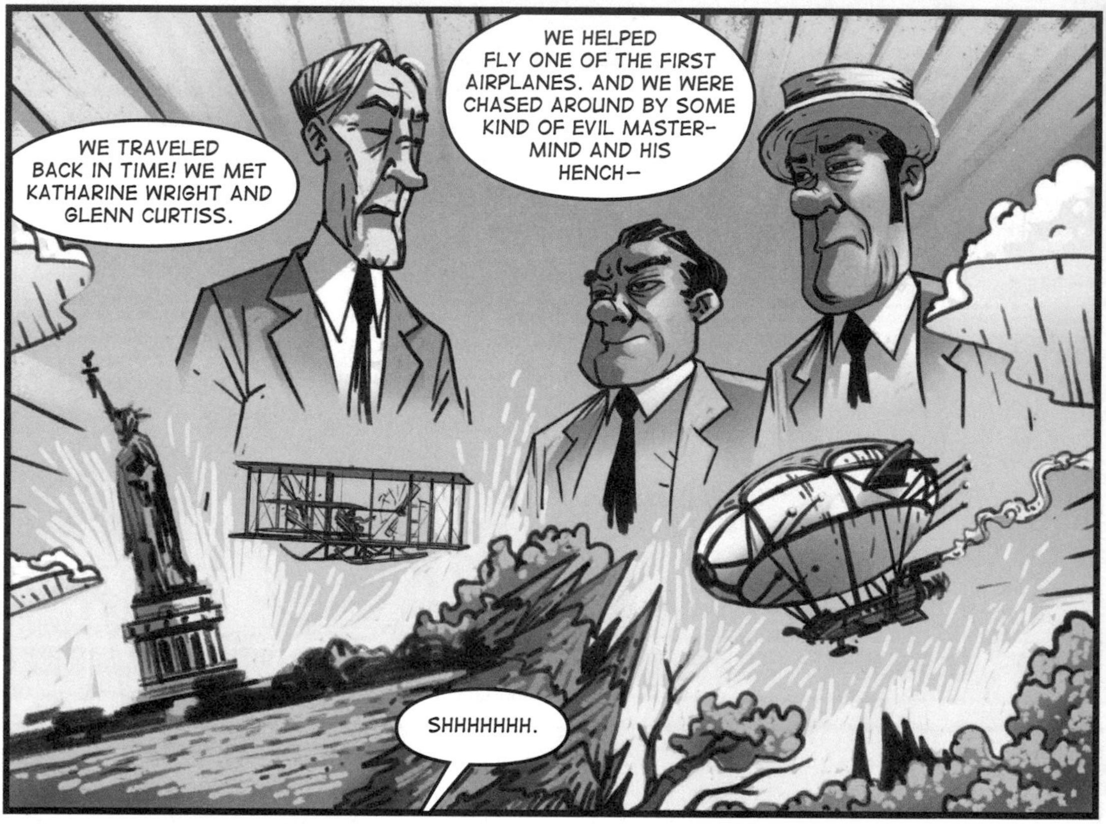
WE TRAVELED BACK IN TIME! WE MET KATHARINE WRIGHT AND GLENN CURTISS.
WE HELPED FLY ONE OF THE FIRST AIRPLANES. AND WE WERE CHASED AROUND BY SOME KIND OF EVIL MASTER-MIND AND HIS HENCH—
SHHHHHHH.

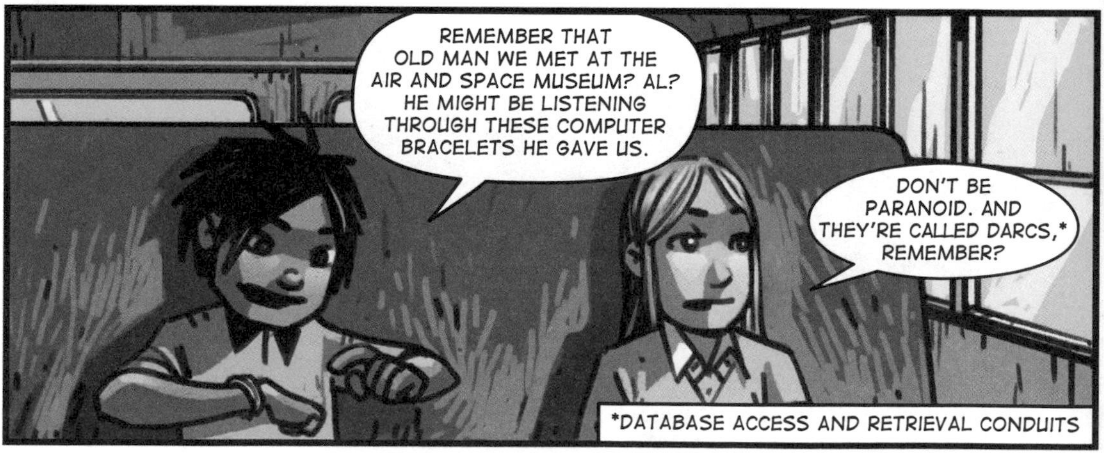
REMEMBER THAT OLD MAN WE MET AT THE AIR AND SPACE MUSEUM? AL? HE MIGHT BE LISTENING THROUGH THESE COMPUTER BRACELETS HE GAVE US.
DON'T BE PARANOID. AND THEY'RE CALLED DARCS,* REMEMBER?
*DATABASE ACCESS AND RETRIEVAL CONDUITS

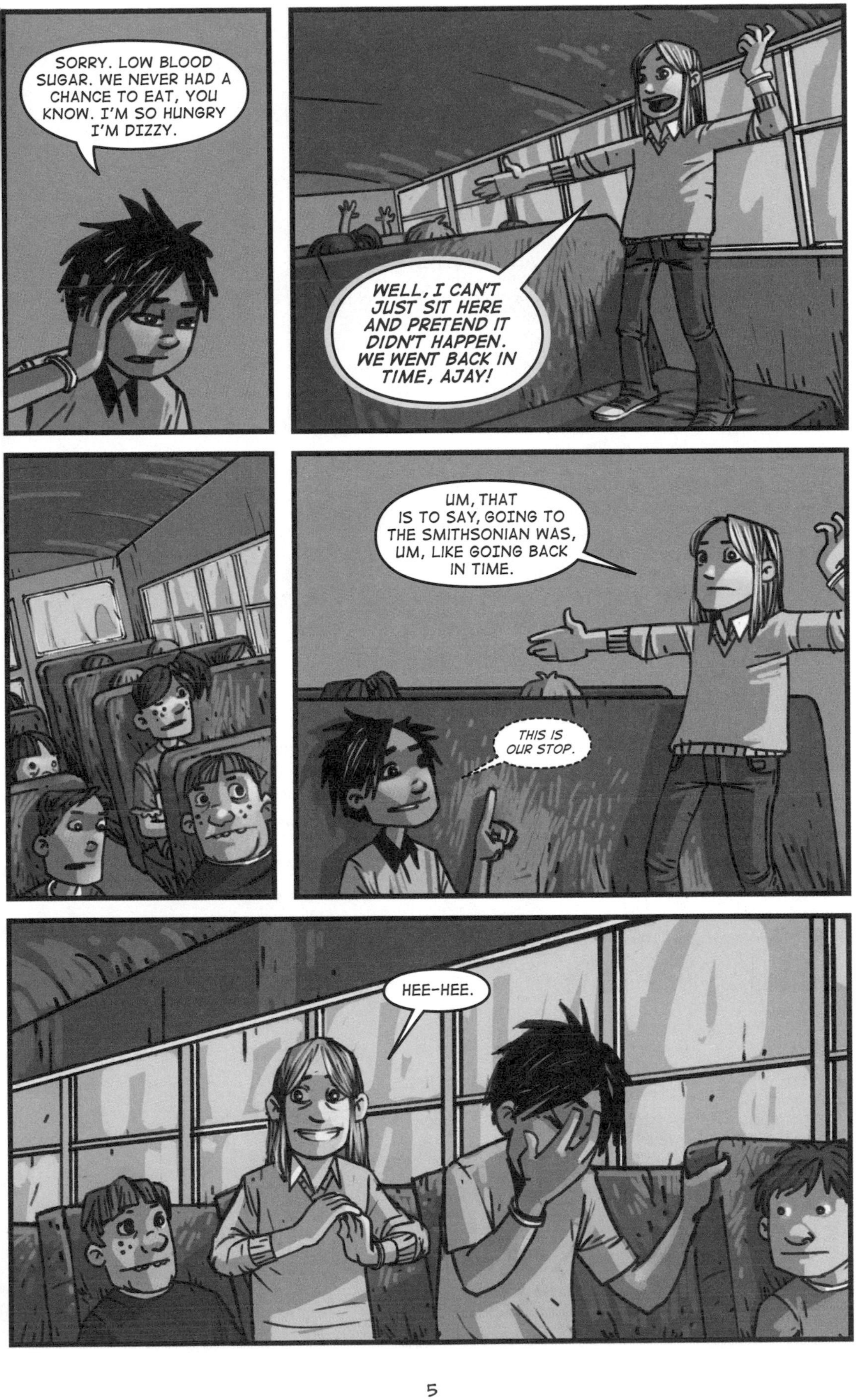
SORRY. LOW BLOOD SUGAR. WE NEVER HAD A CHANCE TO EAT, YOU KNOW. I'M SO HUNGRY I'M DIZZY.
WELL, I CAN'T JUST SIT HERE AND PRETEND IT DIDN'T HAPPEN. WE WENT BACK IN TIME, AJAY!
UM, THAT IS TO SAY, GOING TO THE SMITHSONIAN WAS, UM, LIKE GOING BACK IN TIME.
THIS IS OUR STOP.
HEE-HEE.

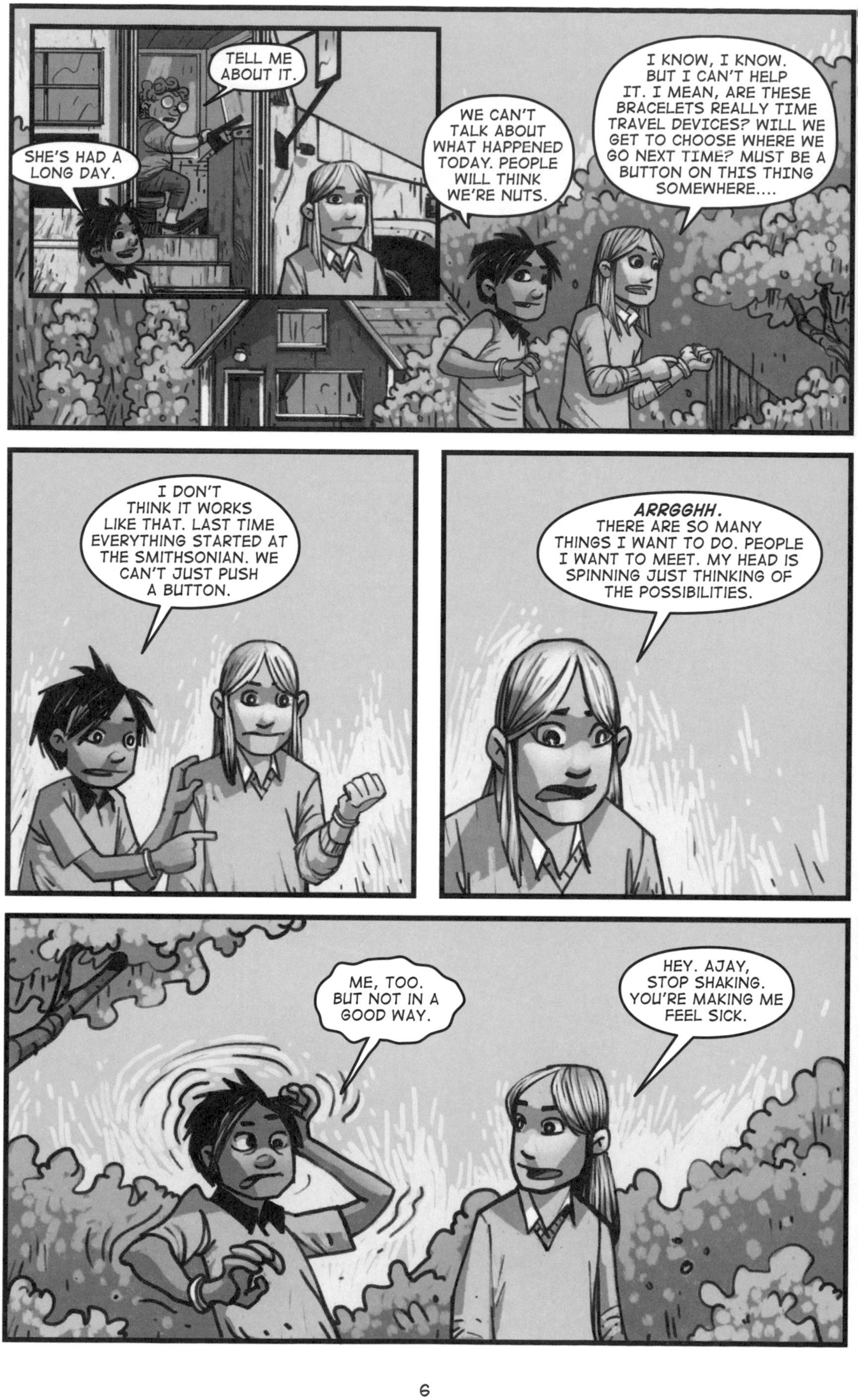
SHE'S HAD A LONG DAY.
TELL ME ABOUT IT.
WE CAN'T TALK ABOUT WHAT HAPPENED TODAY. PEOPLE WILL THINK WE'RE NUTS.
I KNOW, I KNOW. BUT I CAN'T HELP IT. I MEAN, ARE THESE BRACELETS REALLY TIME TRAVEL DEVICES? WILL WE GET TO CHOOSE WHERE WE GO NEXT TIME? MUST BE A BUTTON ON THIS THING SOMEWHERE....
I DON'T THINK IT WORKS LIKE THAT. LAST TIME EVERYTHING STARTED AT THE SMITHSONIAN. WE CAN'T JUST PUSH A BUTTON.
ARRGGHH. THERE ARE SO MANY THINGS I WANT TO DO. PEOPLE I WANT TO MEET. MY HEAD IS SPINNING JUST THINKING OF THE POSSIBILITIES.
ME, TOO. BUT NOT IN A GOOD WAY.
HEY. AJAY, STOP SHAKING. YOU'RE MAKING ME FEEL SICK.

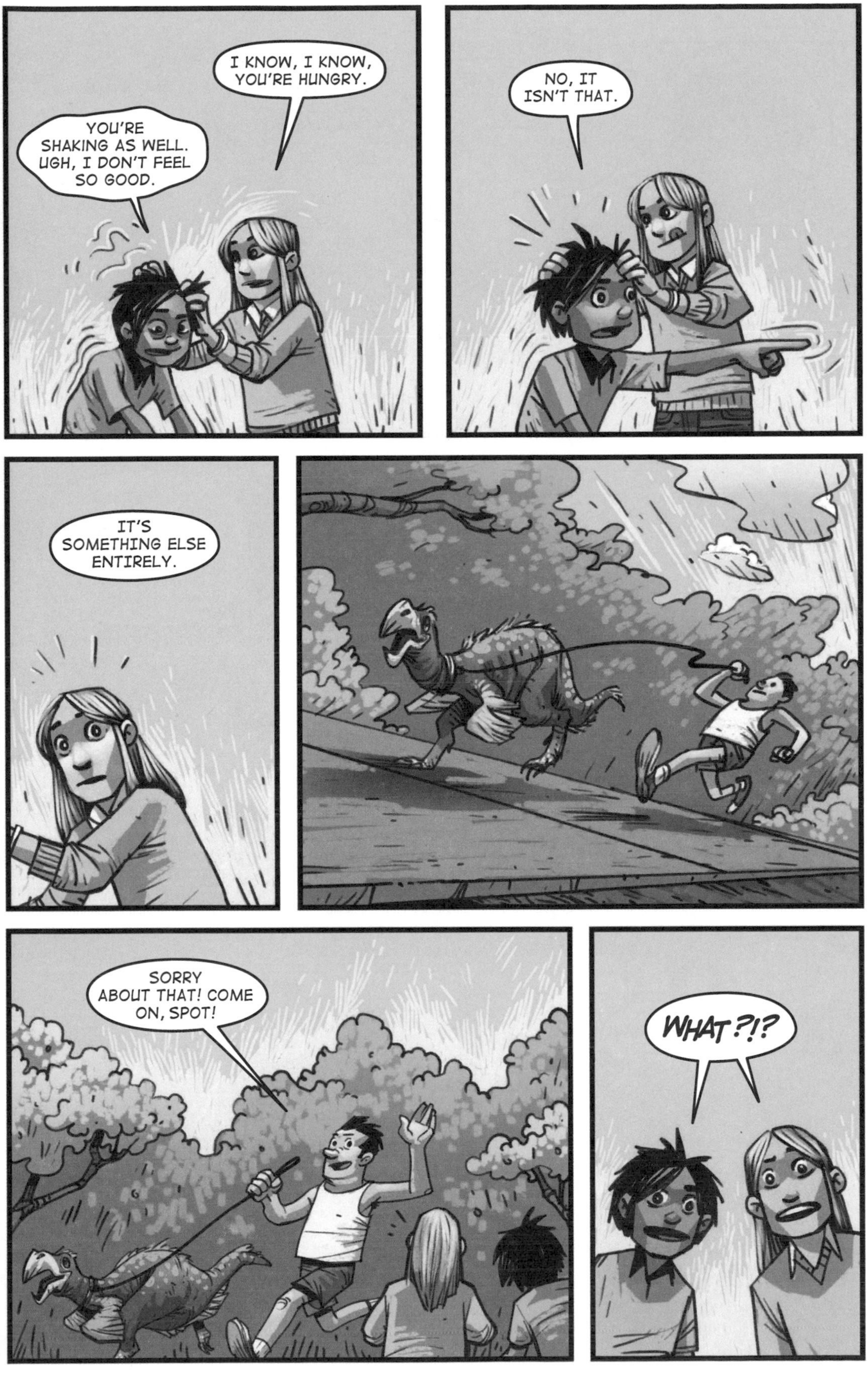
YOU'RE SHAKING AS WELL. UGH, I DON'T FEEL SO GOOD.
I KNOW, I KNOW, YOU'RE HUNGRY.
NO, IT ISN'T THAT.
IT'S SOMETHING ELSE ENTIRELY.
SORRY ABOUT THAT! COME ON, SPOT!
WHAT?!?

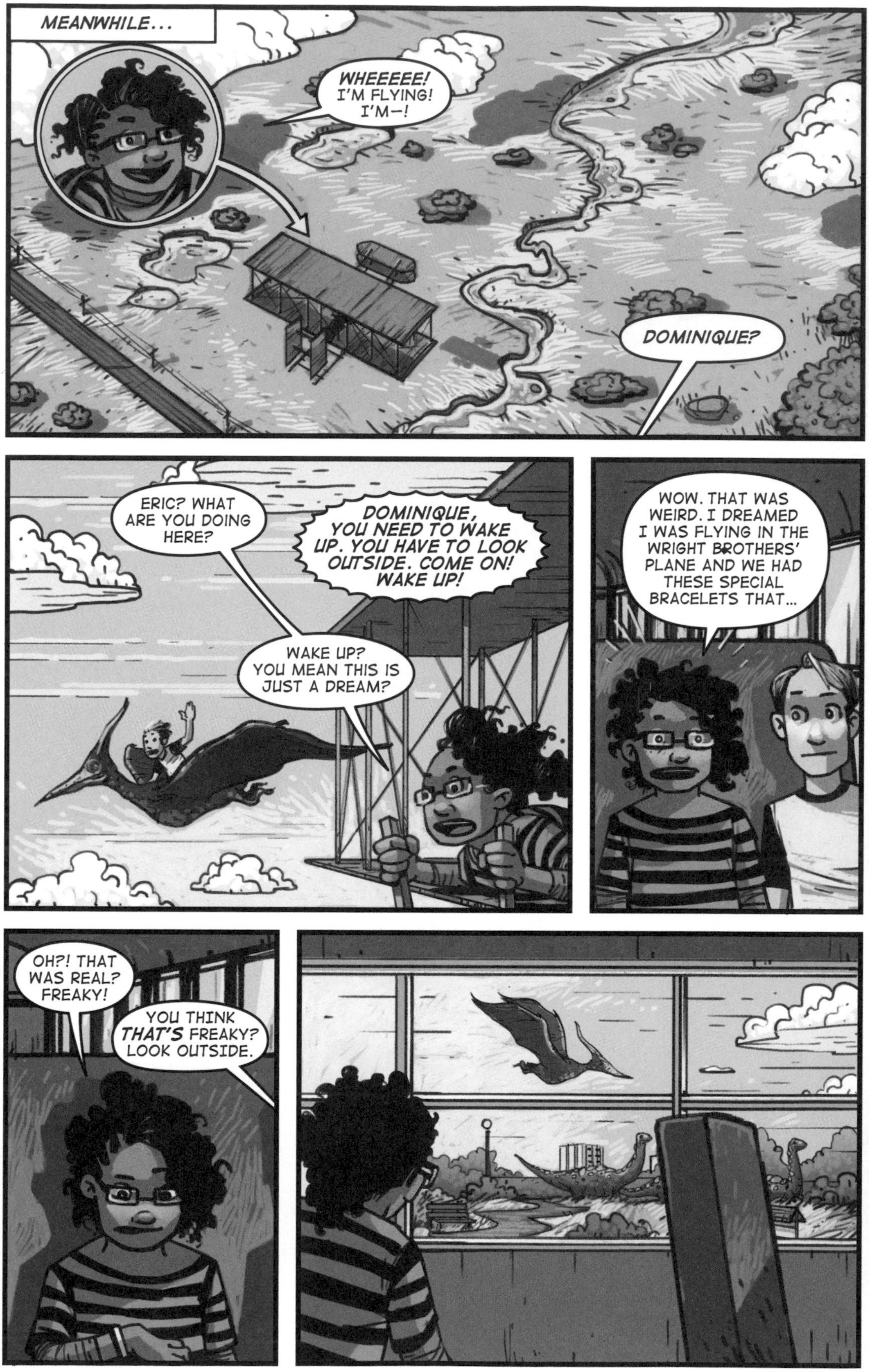
MEANWHILE...
WHEEEEE! I'M FLYING! I'M—!
DOMINIQUE?
ERIC? WHAT ARE YOU DOING HERE?
DOMINIQUE, YOU NEED TO WAKE UP. YOU HAVE TO LOOK OUTSIDE. COME ON! WAKE UP!
WAKE UP? YOU MEAN THIS IS JUST A DREAM?
WOW. THAT WAS WEIRD. I DREAMED I WAS FLYING IN THE WRIGHT BROTHERS' PLANE AND WE HAD THESE SPECIAL BRACELETS THAT...
OH?! THAT WAS REAL? FREAKY!
YOU THINK THAT'S FREAKY? LOOK OUTSIDE.

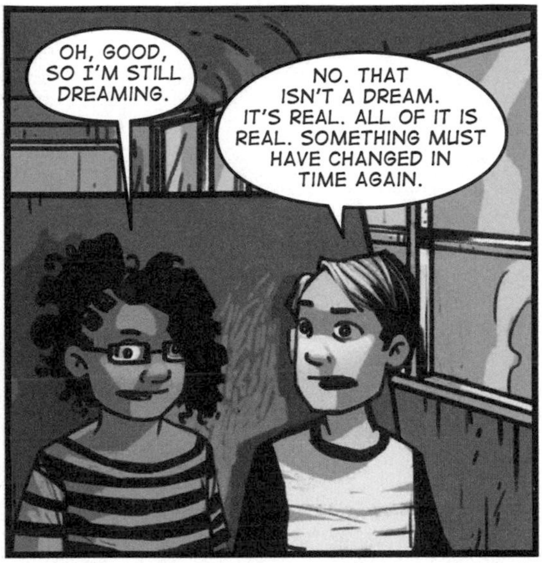
OH, GOOD, SO I'M STILL DREAMING.
NO. THAT ISN'T A DREAM. IT'S REAL. ALL OF IT IS REAL. SOMETHING MUST HAVE CHANGED IN TIME AGAIN.

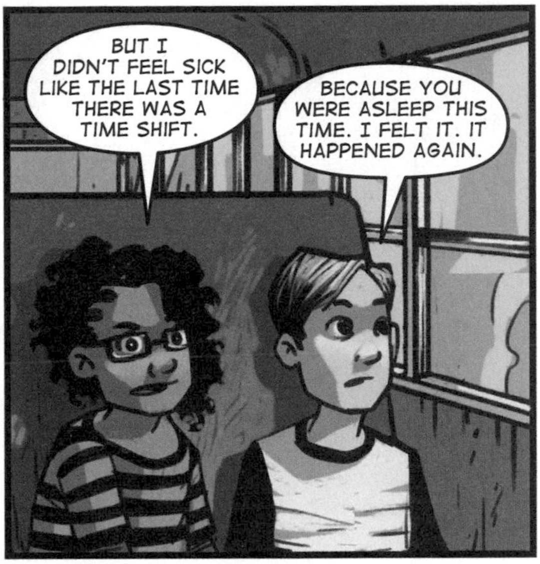
BUT I DIDN'T FEEL SICK LIKE THE LAST TIME THERE WAS A TIME SHIFT.
BECAUSE YOU WERE ASLEEP THIS TIME. I FELT IT. IT HAPPENED AGAIN.

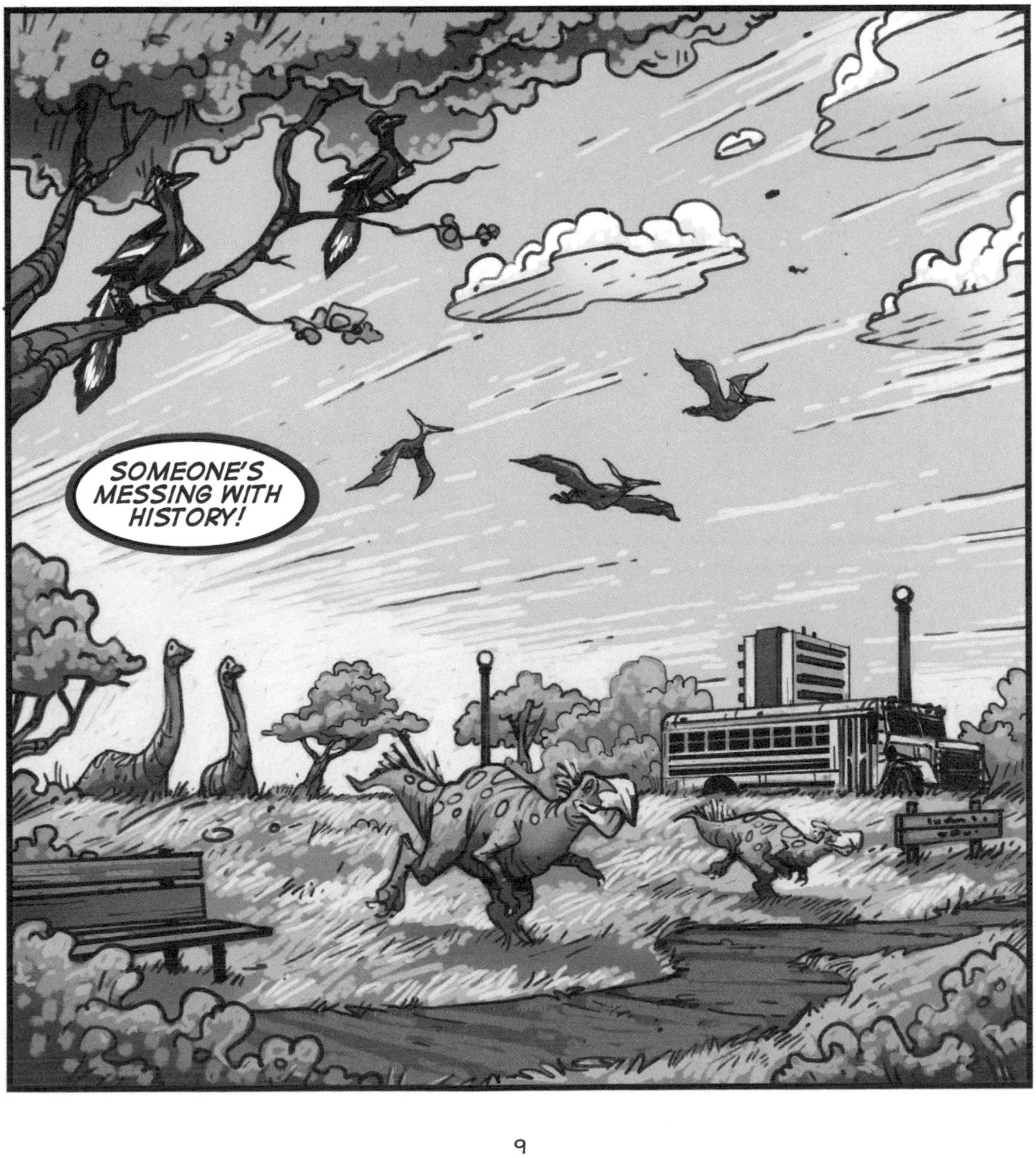
SOMEONE'S MESSING WITH HISTORY!

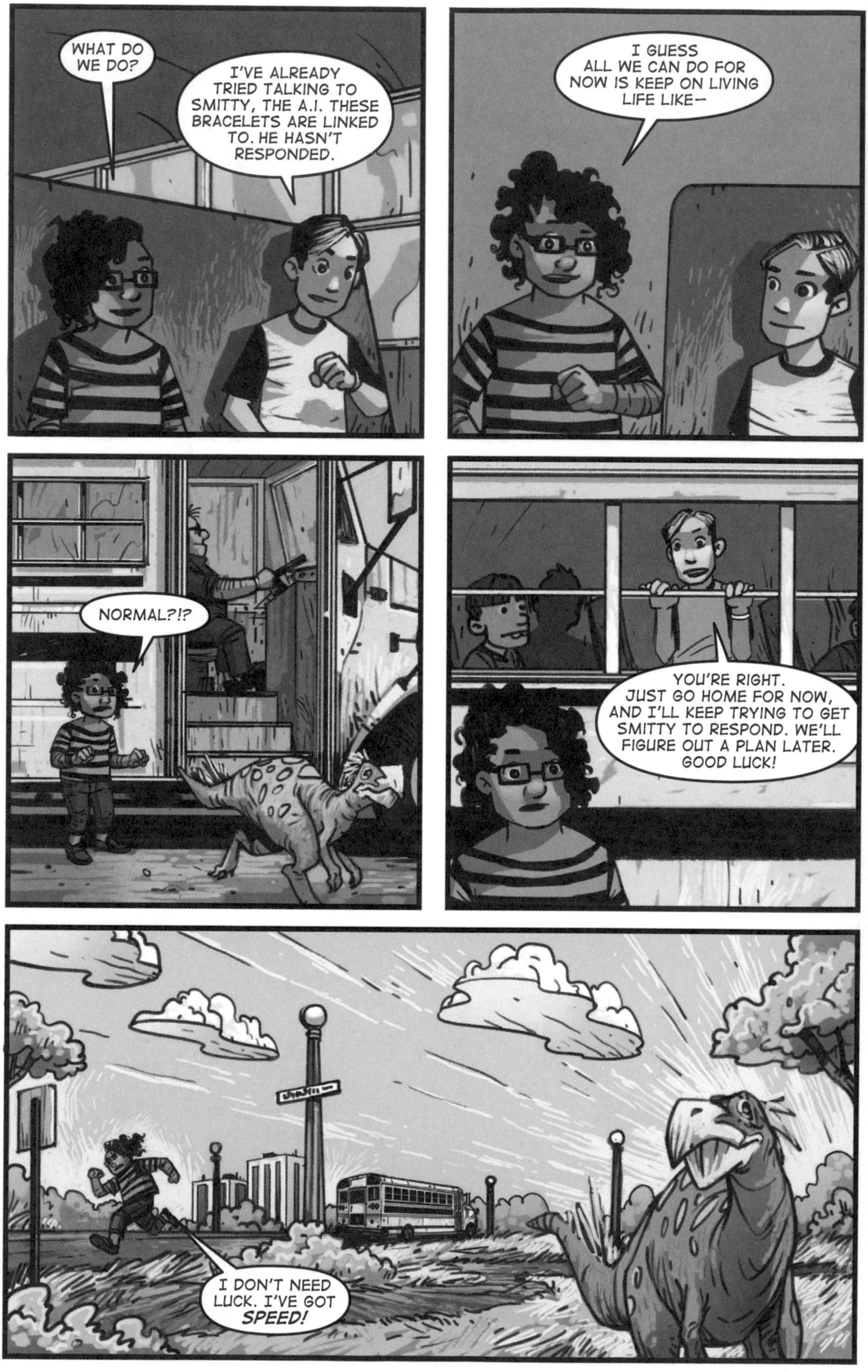
WHAT DO WE DO?
I'VE ALREADY TRIED TALKING TO SMITTY, THE A.I. THESE BRACELETS ARE LINKED TO. HE HASN'T RESPONDED.
I GUESS ALL WE CAN DO FOR NOW IS KEEP ON LIVING LIFE LIKE—
NORMAL?!?
YOU'RE RIGHT. JUST GO HOME FOR NOW, AND I'LL KEEP TRYING TO GET SMITTY TO RESPOND. WE'LL FIGURE OUT A PLAN LATER. GOOD LUCK!
I DON'T NEED LUCK. I'VE GOT *SPEED!*

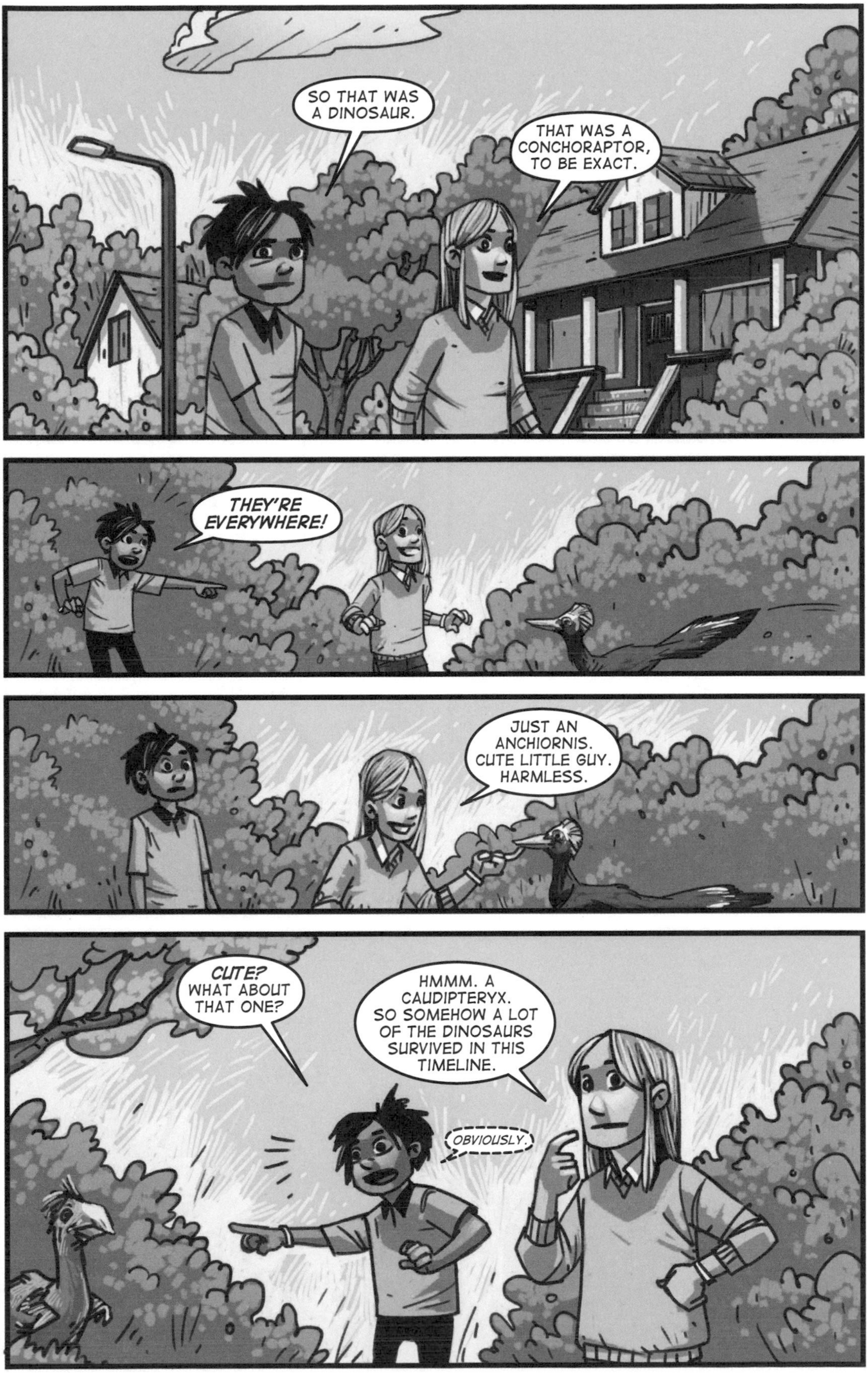
SO THAT WAS A DINOSAUR.
THAT WAS A CONCHORAPTOR, TO BE EXACT.
THEY'RE EVERYWHERE!
JUST AN ANCHIORNIS. CUTE LITTLE GUY. HARMLESS.
CUTE? WHAT ABOUT THAT ONE?
HMMM. A CAUDIPTERYX. SO SOMEHOW A LOT OF THE DINOSAURS SURVIVED IN THIS TIMELINE.
OBVIOUSLY.

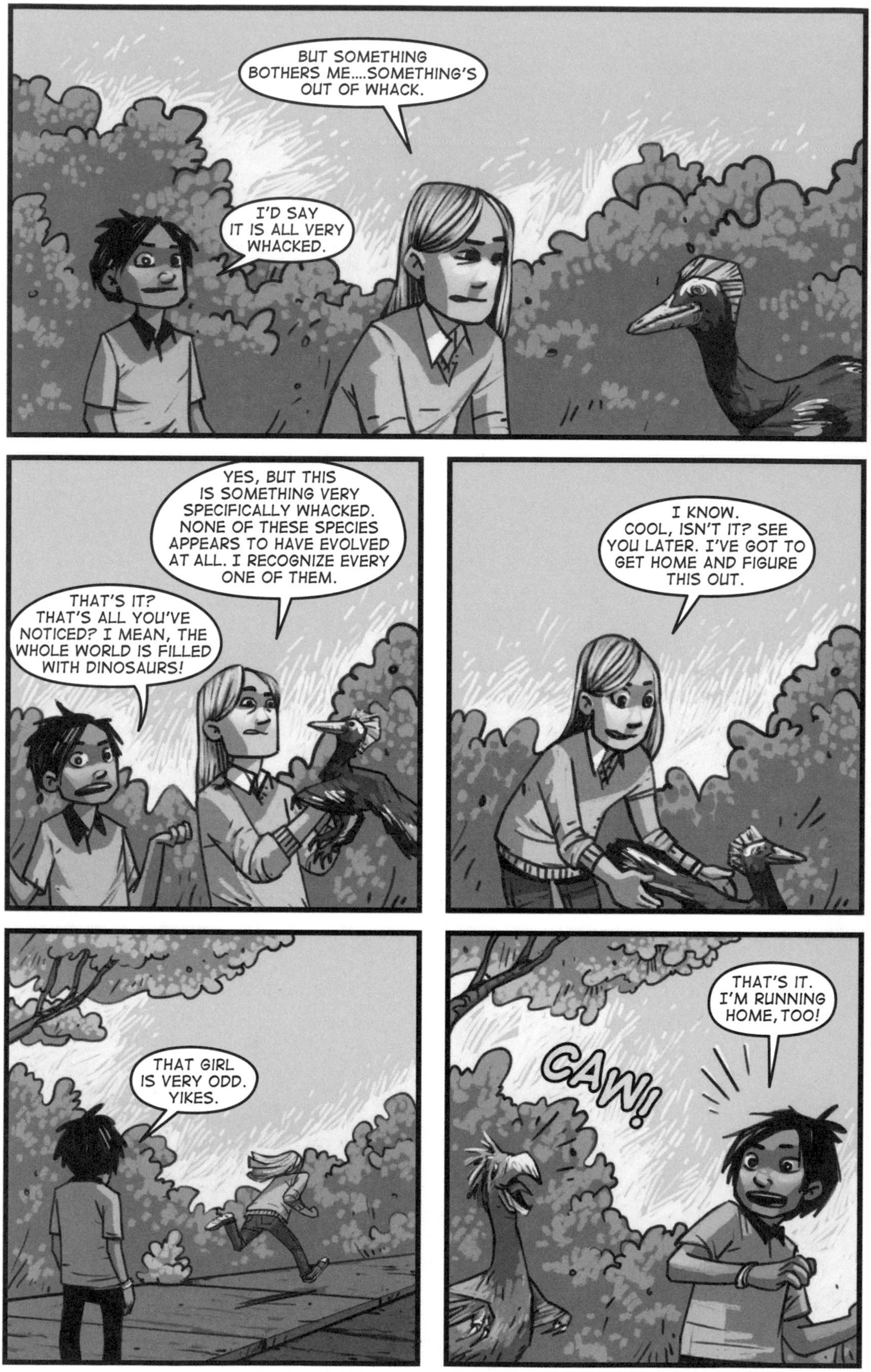
BUT SOMETHING BOTHERS ME....SOMETHING'S OUT OF WHACK.
I'D SAY IT IS ALL VERY WHACKED.
YES, BUT THIS IS SOMETHING VERY SPECIFICALLY WHACKED. NONE OF THESE SPECIES APPEARS TO HAVE EVOLVED AT ALL. I RECOGNIZE EVERY ONE OF THEM.
THAT'S IT? THAT'S ALL YOU'VE NOTICED? I MEAN, THE WHOLE WORLD IS FILLED WITH DINOSAURS!
I KNOW. COOL, ISN'T IT? SEE YOU LATER. I'VE GOT TO GET HOME AND FIGURE THIS OUT.
THAT GIRL IS VERY ODD. YIKES.
CAW!
THAT'S IT. I'M RUNNING HOME, TOO!

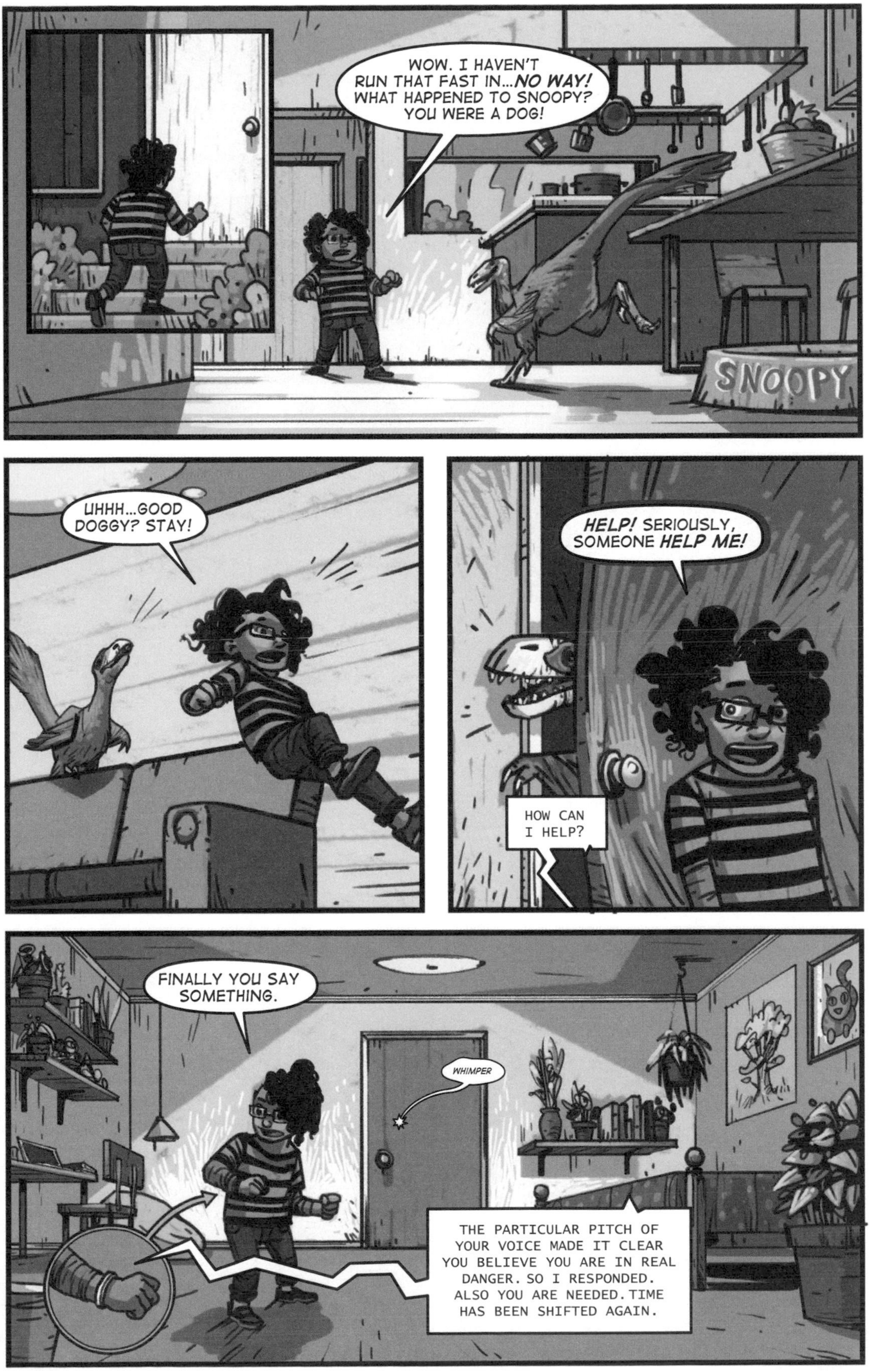
WOW. I HAVEN'T RUN THAT FAST IN...NO WAY! WHAT HAPPENED TO SNOOPY? YOU WERE A DOG!
SNOOPY
UHHH...GOOD DOGGY? STAY!
HELP! SERIOUSLY, SOMEONE HELP ME!
HOW CAN I HELP?
FINALLY YOU SAY SOMETHING.
WHIMPER
THE PARTICULAR PITCH OF YOUR VOICE MADE IT CLEAR YOU BELIEVE YOU ARE IN REAL DANGER. SO I RESPONDED. ALSO YOU ARE NEEDED. TIME HAS BEEN SHIFTED AGAIN.

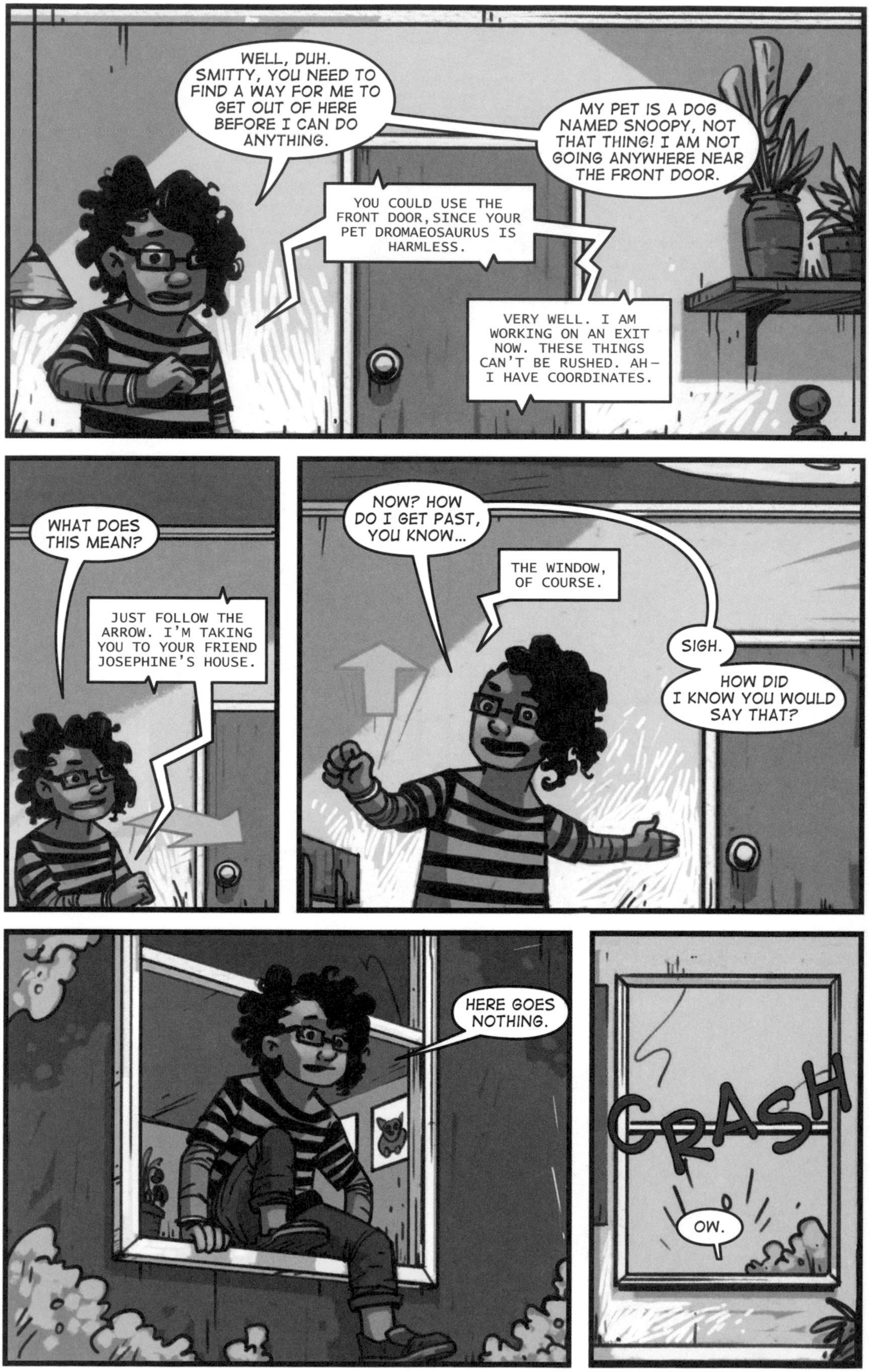
WELL, DUH. SMITTY, YOU NEED TO FIND A WAY FOR ME TO GET OUT OF HERE BEFORE I CAN DO ANYTHING.
YOU COULD USE THE FRONT DOOR, SINCE YOUR PET DROMAEOSAURUS IS HARMLESS.
MY PET IS A DOG NAMED SNOOPY, NOT THAT THING! I AM NOT GOING ANYWHERE NEAR THE FRONT DOOR.
VERY WELL. I AM WORKING ON AN EXIT NOW. THESE THINGS CAN'T BE RUSHED. AH– I HAVE COORDINATES.
WHAT DOES THIS MEAN?
JUST FOLLOW THE ARROW. I'M TAKING YOU TO YOUR FRIEND JOSEPHINE'S HOUSE.
NOW? HOW DO I GET PAST, YOU KNOW...
THE WINDOW, OF COURSE.
SIGH.
HOW DID I KNOW YOU WOULD SAY THAT?
HERE GOES NOTHING.
CRASH
OW.

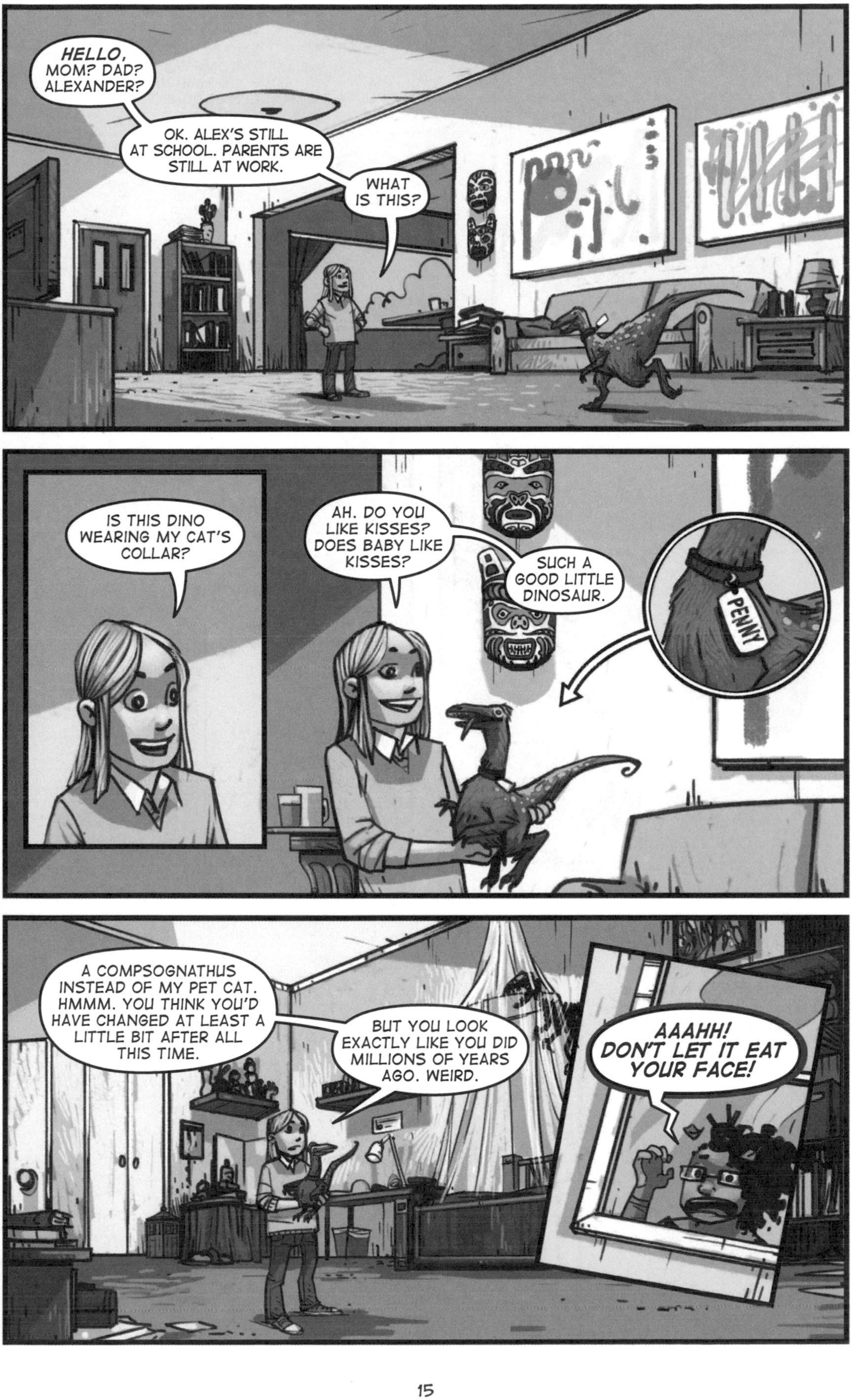
HELLO, MOM? DAD? ALEXANDER?
OK. ALEX'S STILL AT SCHOOL. PARENTS ARE STILL AT WORK.
WHAT IS THIS?
IS THIS DINO WEARING MY CAT'S COLLAR?
AH. DO YOU LIKE KISSES? DOES BABY LIKE KISSES?
SUCH A GOOD LITTLE DINOSAUR.
PENNY
A COMPSOGNATHUS INSTEAD OF MY PET CAT. HMMM. YOU THINK YOU'D HAVE CHANGED AT LEAST A LITTLE BIT AFTER ALL THIS TIME.
BUT YOU LOOK EXACTLY LIKE YOU DID MILLIONS OF YEARS AGO. WEIRD.
AAAHH! DON'T LET IT EAT YOUR FACE!

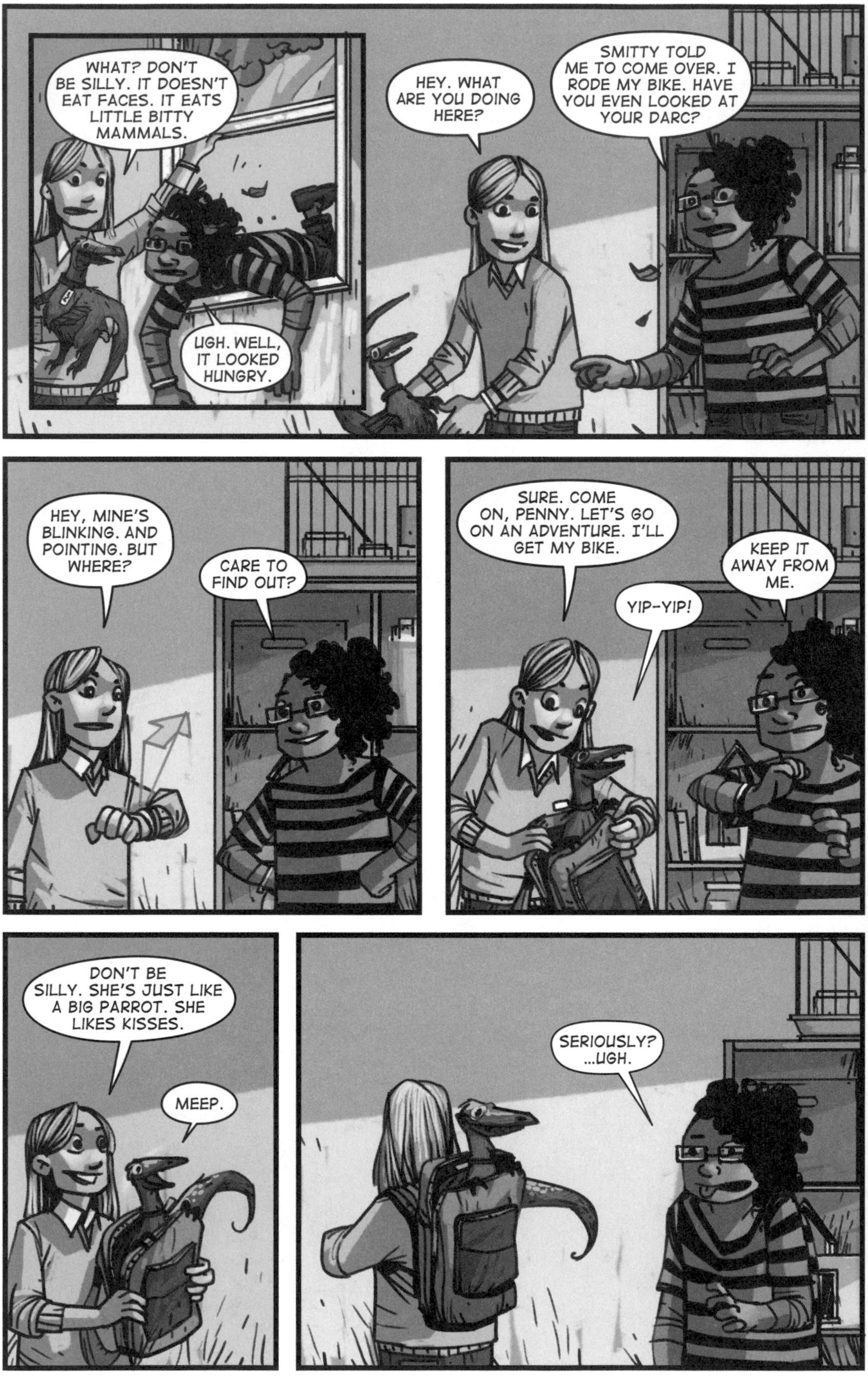
WHAT? DON'T BE SILLY. IT DOESN'T EAT FACES. IT EATS LITTLE BITTY MAMMALS.
UGH. WELL, IT LOOKED HUNGRY.
HEY. WHAT ARE YOU DOING HERE?
SMITTY TOLD ME TO COME OVER. I RODE MY BIKE. HAVE YOU EVEN LOOKED AT YOUR DARC?
HEY, MINE'S BLINKING. AND POINTING. BUT WHERE?
CARE TO FIND OUT?
SURE. COME ON, PENNY. LET'S GO ON AN ADVENTURE. I'LL GET MY BIKE.
YIP-YIP!
KEEP IT AWAY FROM ME.
DON'T BE SILLY. SHE'S JUST LIKE A BIG PARROT. SHE LIKES KISSES.
MEEP.
SERIOUSLY? ...UGH.

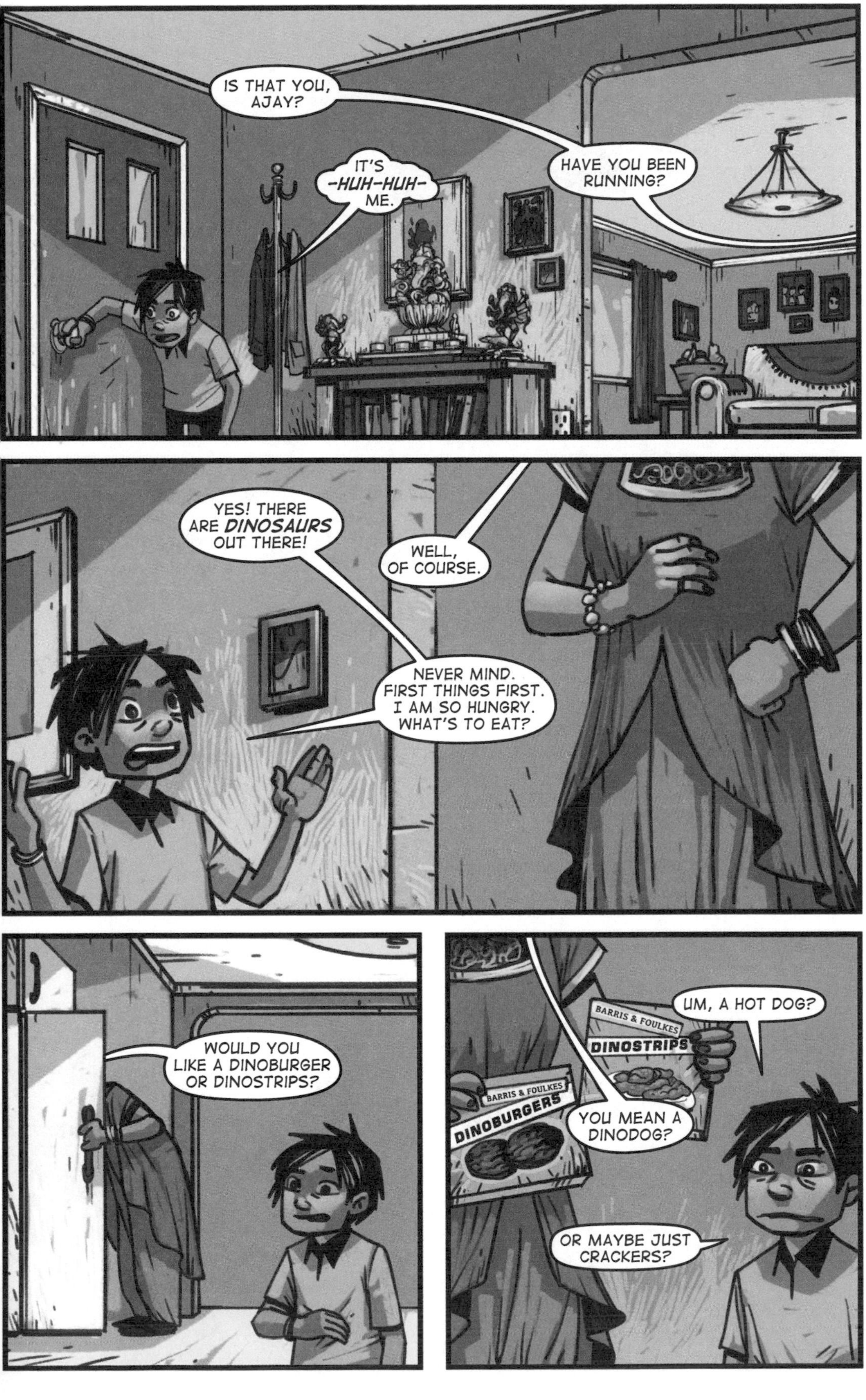
IS THAT YOU, AJAY?
IT'S -HUH-HUH- ME.
HAVE YOU BEEN RUNNING?
YES! THERE ARE DINOSAURS OUT THERE!
WELL, OF COURSE.
NEVER MIND. FIRST THINGS FIRST. I AM SO HUNGRY. WHAT'S TO EAT?
WOULD YOU LIKE A DINOBURGER OR DINOSTRIPS?
BARRIS & FOULKES
DINOSTRIPS
UM, A HOT DOG?
BARRIS & FOULKES
DINOBURGERS
YOU MEAN A DINODOG?
OR MAYBE JUST CRACKERS?

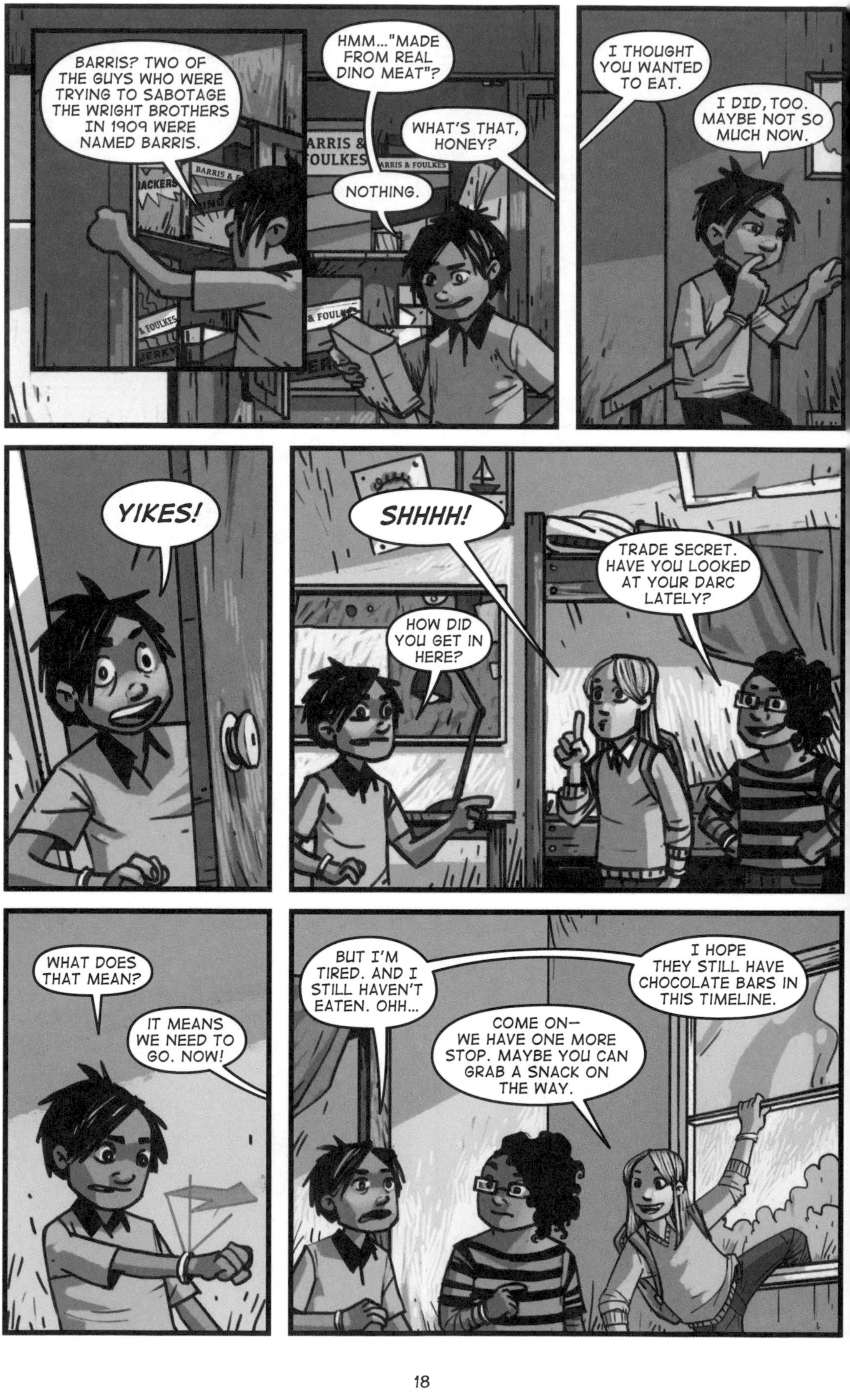

BARRIS? TWO OF THE GUYS WHO WERE TRYING TO SABOTAGE THE WRIGHT BROTHERS IN 1909 WERE NAMED BARRIS.
BARRIS & FOULKES
HMM..."MADE FROM REAL DINO MEAT"?
WHAT'S THAT, HONEY?
NOTHING.
I THOUGHT YOU WANTED TO EAT.
I DID, TOO. MAYBE NOT SO MUCH NOW.
YIKES!
SHHHH!
HOW DID YOU GET IN HERE?
TRADE SECRET. HAVE YOU LOOKED AT YOUR DARC LATELY?
WHAT DOES THAT MEAN?
IT MEANS WE NEED TO GO. NOW!
BUT I'M TIRED. AND I STILL HAVEN'T EATEN. OHH...
I HOPE THEY STILL HAVE CHOCOLATE BARS IN THIS TIMELINE.
COME ON— WE HAVE ONE MORE STOP. MAYBE YOU CAN GRAB A SNACK ON THE WAY.

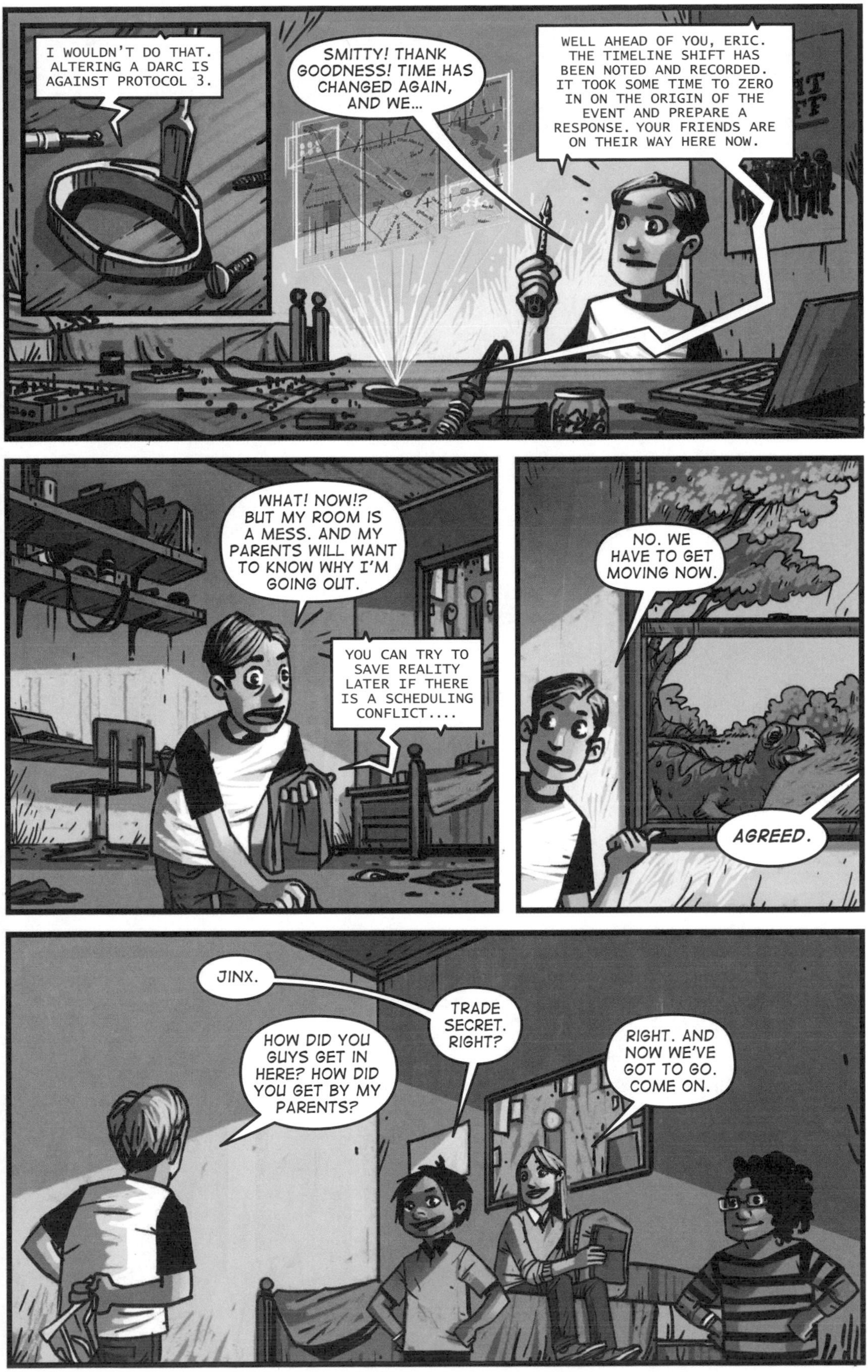
I WOULDN'T DO THAT. ALTERING A DARC IS AGAINST PROTOCOL 3.
SMITTY! THANK GOODNESS! TIME HAS CHANGED AGAIN, AND WE...
WELL AHEAD OF YOU, ERIC. THE TIMELINE SHIFT HAS BEEN NOTED AND RECORDED. IT TOOK SOME TIME TO ZERO IN ON THE ORIGIN OF THE EVENT AND PREPARE A RESPONSE. YOUR FRIENDS ARE ON THEIR WAY HERE NOW.
WHAT! NOW!? BUT MY ROOM IS A MESS. AND MY PARENTS WILL WANT TO KNOW WHY I'M GOING OUT.
YOU CAN TRY TO SAVE REALITY LATER IF THERE IS A SCHEDULING CONFLICT....
NO. WE HAVE TO GET MOVING NOW.
AGREED.
JINX.
HOW DID YOU GUYS GET IN HERE? HOW DID YOU GET BY MY PARENTS?
TRADE SECRET. RIGHT?
RIGHT. AND NOW WE'VE GOT TO GO. COME ON.

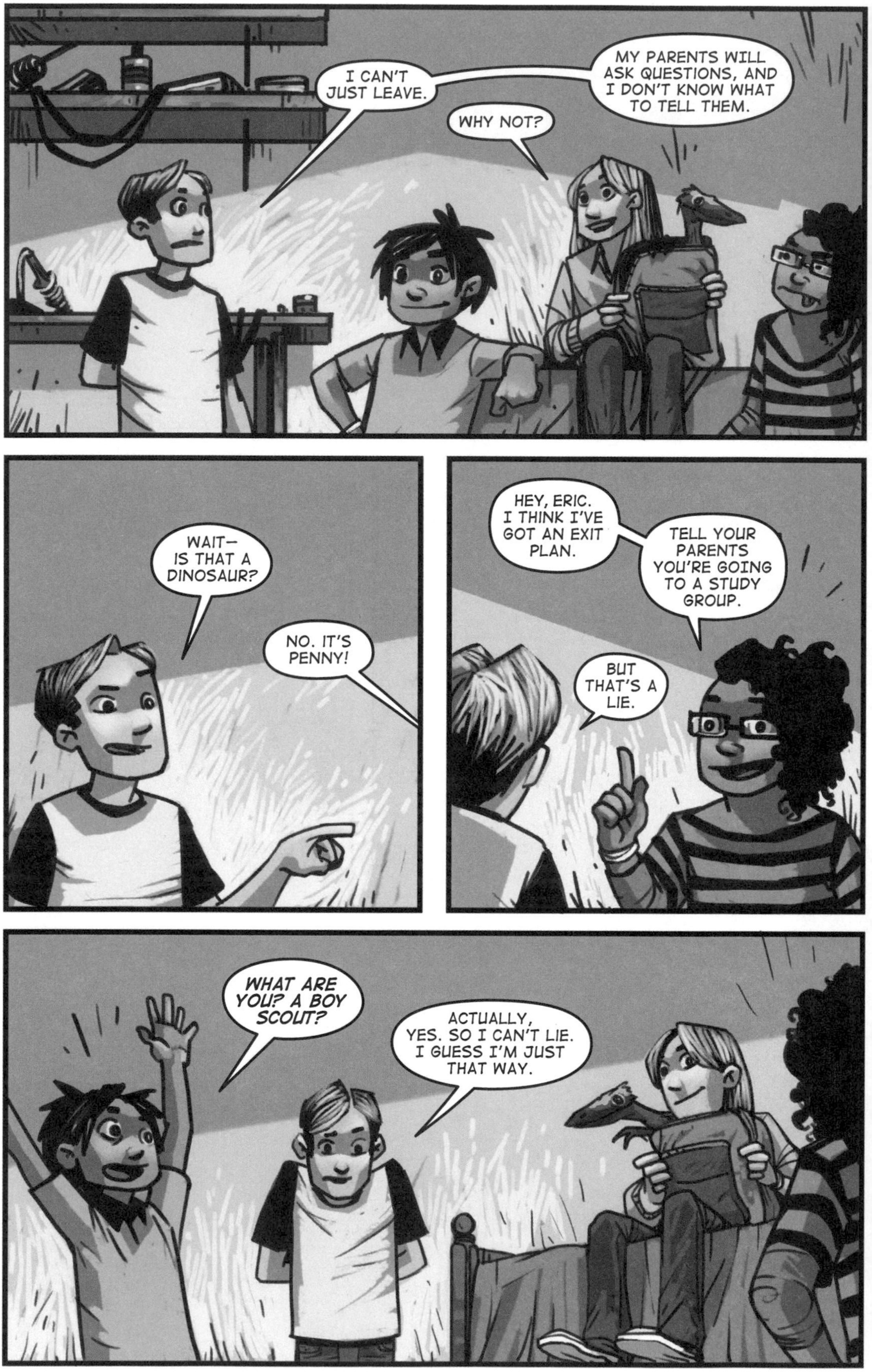
I CAN'T JUST LEAVE.
MY PARENTS WILL ASK QUESTIONS, AND I DON'T KNOW WHAT TO TELL THEM.
WHY NOT?
WAIT— IS THAT A DINOSAUR?
NO. IT'S PENNY!
HEY, ERIC. I THINK I'VE GOT AN EXIT PLAN.
TELL YOUR PARENTS YOU'RE GOING TO A STUDY GROUP.
BUT THAT'S A LIE.
WHAT ARE YOU? A BOY SCOUT?
ACTUALLY, YES. SO I CAN'T LIE. I GUESS I'M JUST THAT WAY.

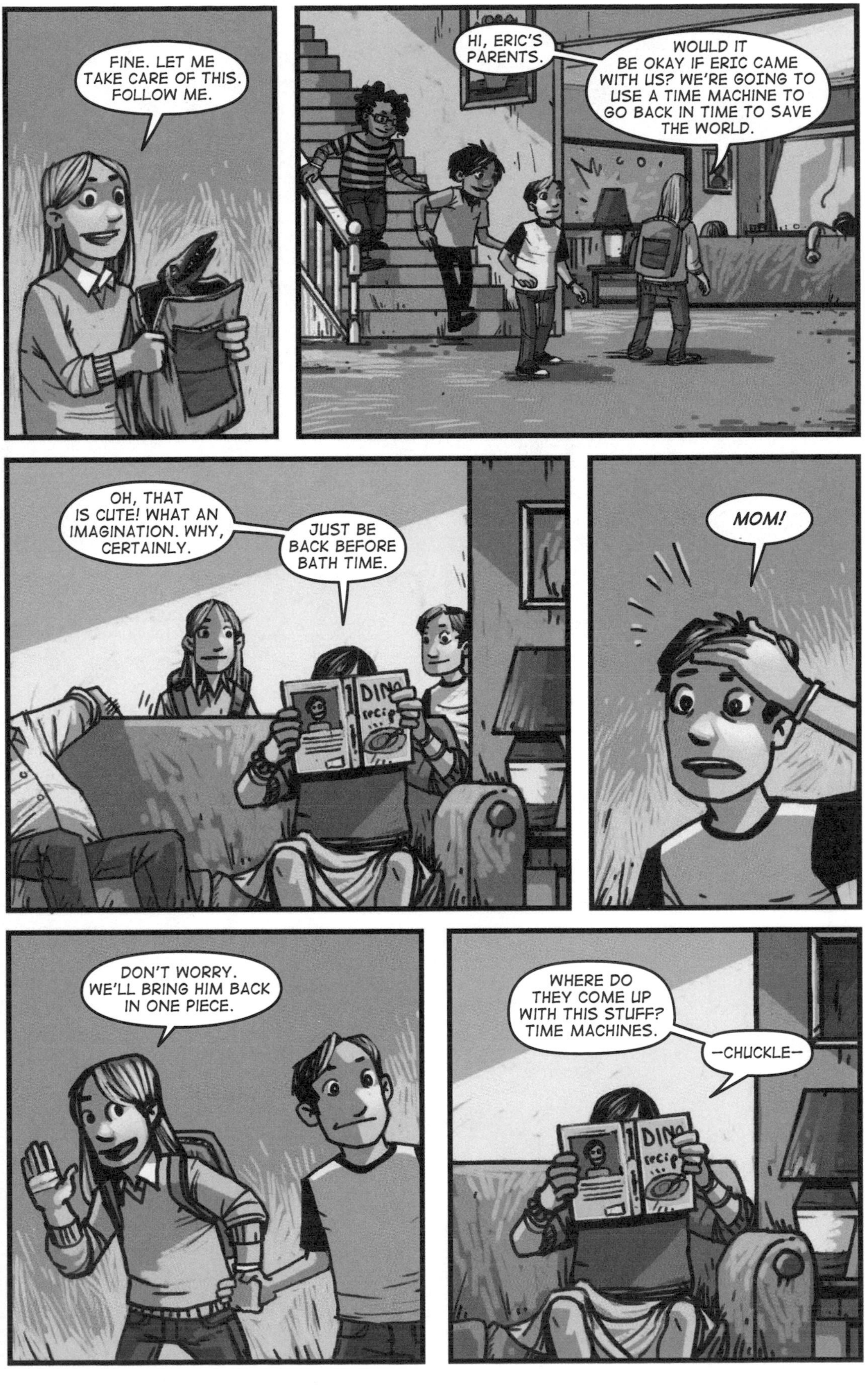

FINE. LET ME TAKE CARE OF THIS. FOLLOW ME.
HI, ERIC'S PARENTS.
WOULD IT BE OKAY IF ERIC CAME WITH US? WE'RE GOING TO USE A TIME MACHINE TO GO BACK IN TIME TO SAVE THE WORLD.
OH, THAT IS CUTE! WHAT AN IMAGINATION. WHY, CERTAINLY.
JUST BE BACK BEFORE BATH TIME.
DINO recip
MOM!
DON'T WORRY. WE'LL BRING HIM BACK IN ONE PIECE.
WHERE DO THEY COME UP WITH THIS STUFF? TIME MACHINES.
—CHUCKLE—
DINO recip

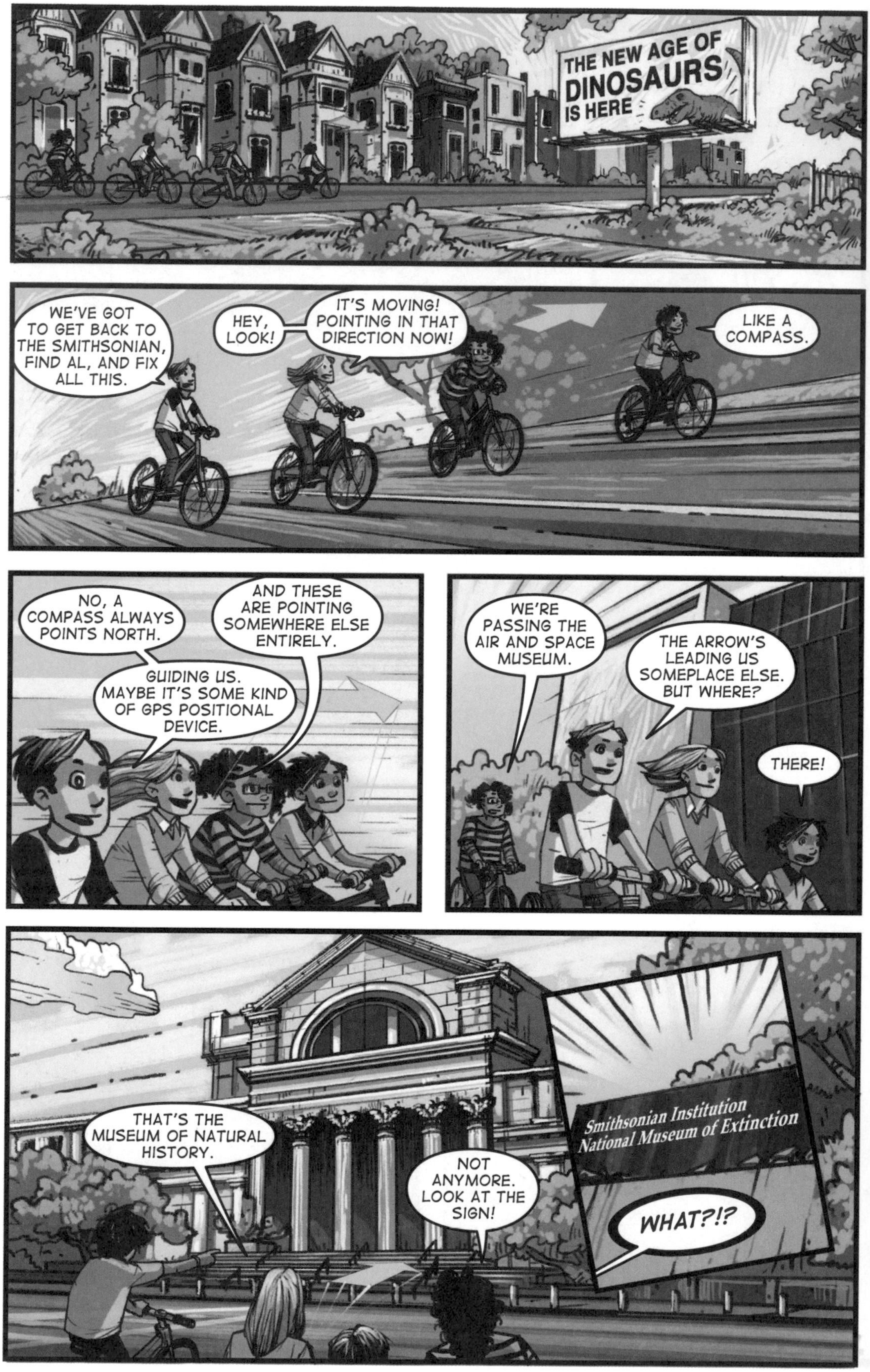
THE NEW AGE OF DINOSAURS IS HERE
WE'VE GOT TO GET BACK TO THE SMITHSONIAN, FIND AL, AND FIX ALL THIS.
HEY, LOOK!
IT'S MOVING! POINTING IN THAT DIRECTION NOW!
LIKE A COMPASS.
NO, A COMPASS ALWAYS POINTS NORTH.
AND THESE ARE POINTING SOMEWHERE ELSE ENTIRELY.
GUIDING US. MAYBE IT'S SOME KIND OF GPS POSITIONAL DEVICE.
WE'RE PASSING THE AIR AND SPACE MUSEUM.
THE ARROW'S LEADING US SOMEPLACE ELSE. BUT WHERE?
THERE!
THAT'S THE MUSEUM OF NATURAL HISTORY.
NOT ANYMORE. LOOK AT THE SIGN!
Smithsonian Institution
National Museum of Extinction
WHAT?!?

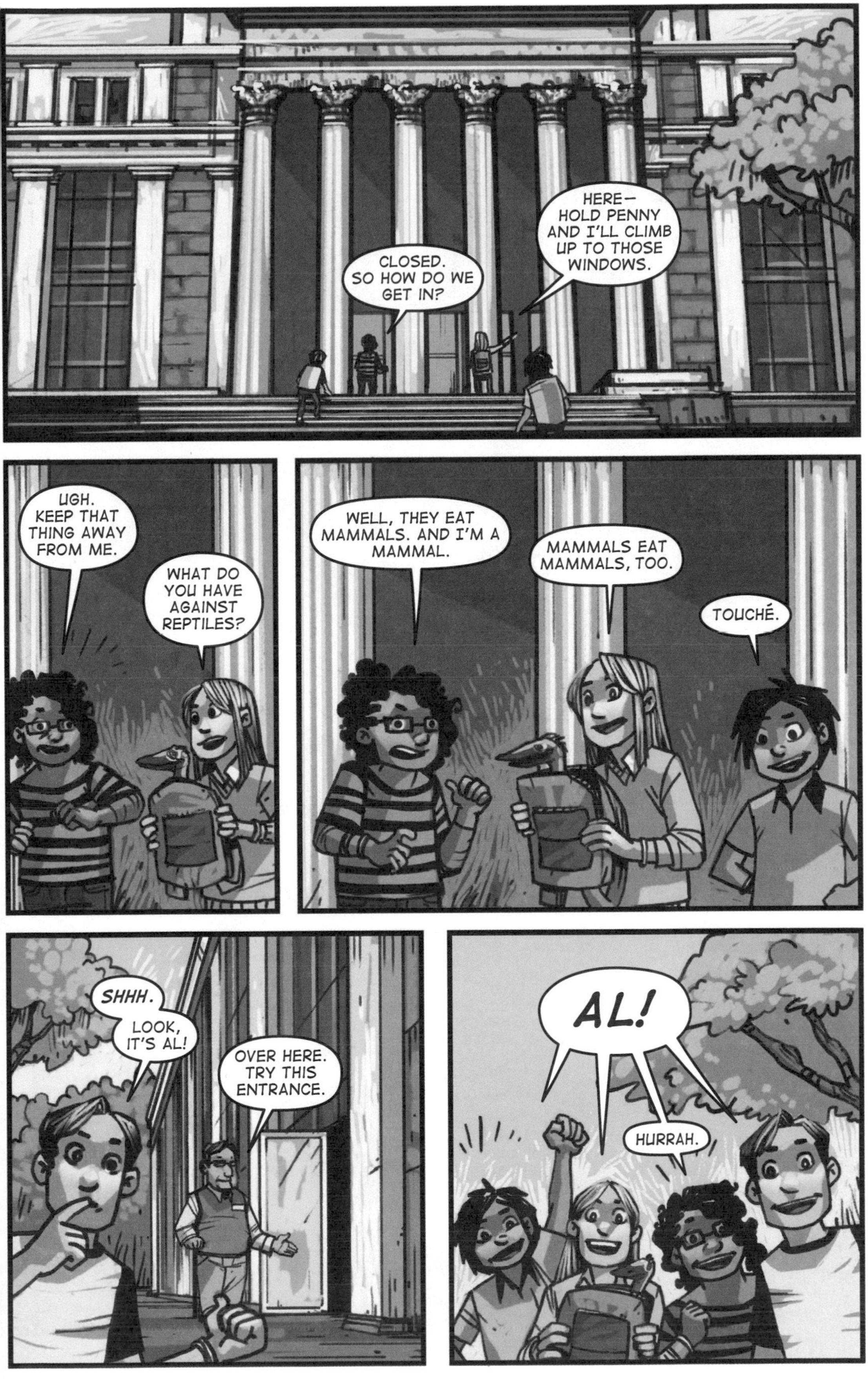
CLOSED. SO HOW DO WE GET IN?
HERE— HOLD PENNY AND I'LL CLIMB UP TO THOSE WINDOWS.
UGH. KEEP THAT THING AWAY FROM ME.
WHAT DO YOU HAVE AGAINST REPTILES?
WELL, THEY EAT MAMMALS. AND I'M A MAMMAL.
MAMMALS EAT MAMMALS, TOO.
TOUCHÉ.
SHHH.
LOOK, IT'S AL!
OVER HERE. TRY THIS ENTRANCE.
AL!
HURRAH.

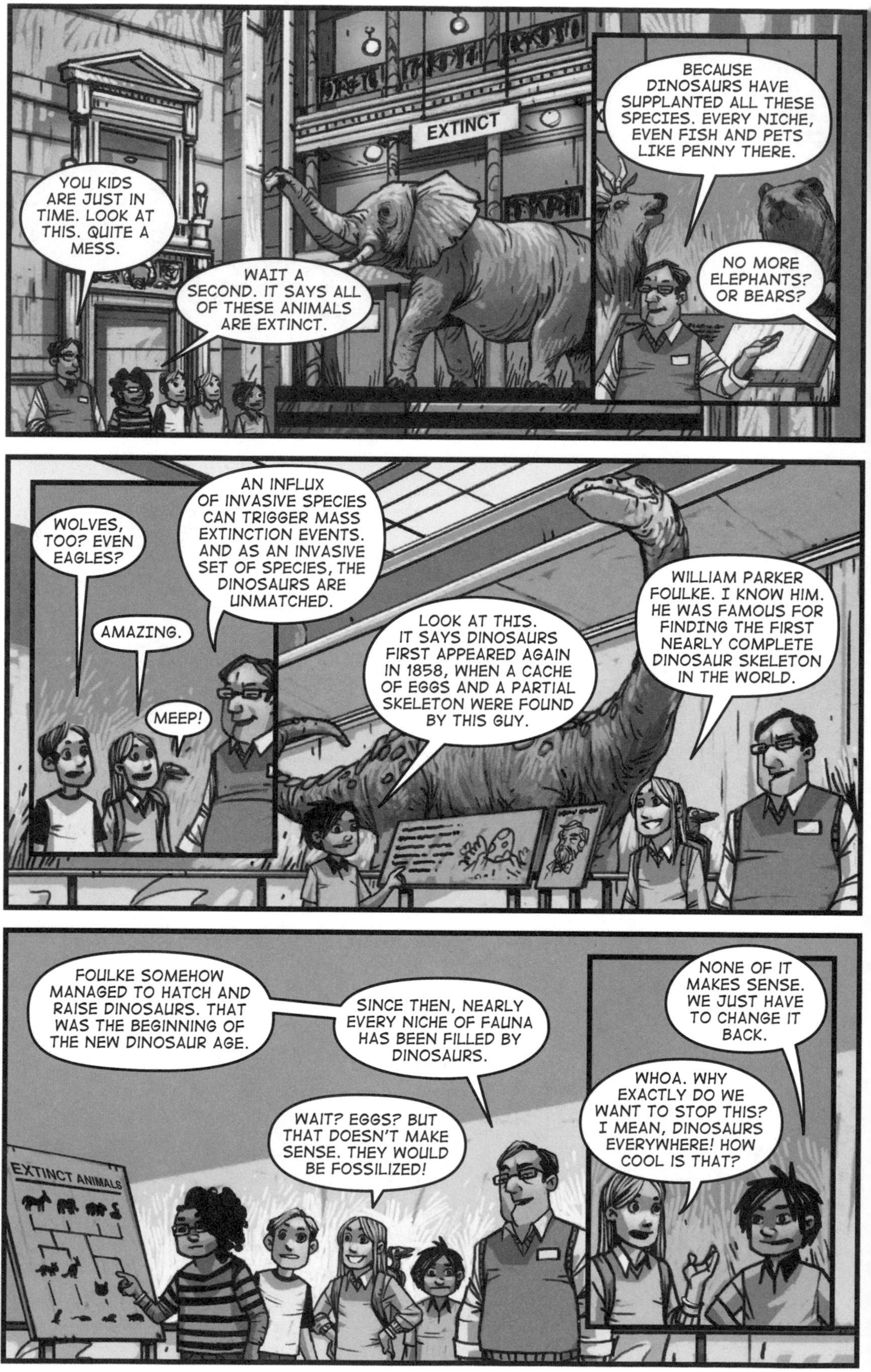
YOU KIDS ARE JUST IN TIME. LOOK AT THIS. QUITE A MESS.
EXTINCT
WAIT A SECOND. IT SAYS ALL OF THESE ANIMALS ARE EXTINCT.
BECAUSE DINOSAURS HAVE SUPPLANTED ALL THESE SPECIES. EVERY NICHE, EVEN FISH AND PETS LIKE PENNY THERE.
NO MORE ELEPHANTS? OR BEARS?
WOLVES, TOO? EVEN EAGLES?
AN INFLUX OF INVASIVE SPECIES CAN TRIGGER MASS EXTINCTION EVENTS. AND AS AN INVASIVE SET OF SPECIES, THE DINOSAURS ARE UNMATCHED.
AMAZING.
MEEP!
LOOK AT THIS. IT SAYS DINOSAURS FIRST APPEARED AGAIN IN 1858, WHEN A CACHE OF EGGS AND A PARTIAL SKELETON WERE FOUND BY THIS GUY.
WILLIAM PARKER FOULKE. I KNOW HIM. HE WAS FAMOUS FOR FINDING THE FIRST NEARLY COMPLETE DINOSAUR SKELETON IN THE WORLD.
FOULKE SOMEHOW MANAGED TO HATCH AND RAISE DINOSAURS. THAT WAS THE BEGINNING OF THE NEW DINOSAUR AGE.
SINCE THEN, NEARLY EVERY NICHE OF FAUNA HAS BEEN FILLED BY DINOSAURS.
EXTINCT ANIMALS
WAIT? EGGS? BUT THAT DOESN'T MAKE SENSE. THEY WOULD BE FOSSILIZED!
NONE OF IT MAKES SENSE. WE JUST HAVE TO CHANGE IT BACK.
WHOA. WHY EXACTLY DO WE WANT TO STOP THIS? I MEAN, DINOSAURS EVERYWHERE! HOW COOL IS THAT?

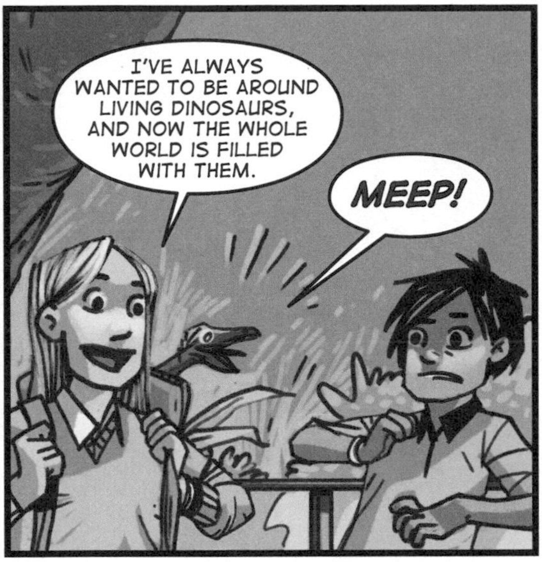
I'VE ALWAYS WANTED TO BE AROUND LIVING DINOSAURS, AND NOW THE WHOLE WORLD IS FILLED WITH THEM.
MEEP!

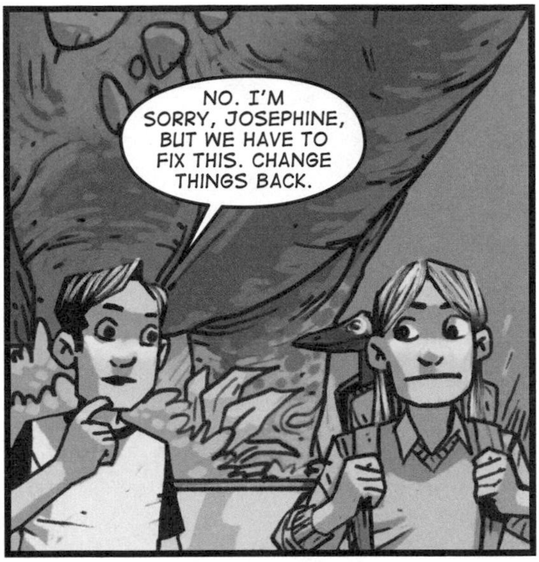
NO. I'M SORRY, JOSEPHINE, BUT WE HAVE TO FIX THIS. CHANGE THINGS BACK.

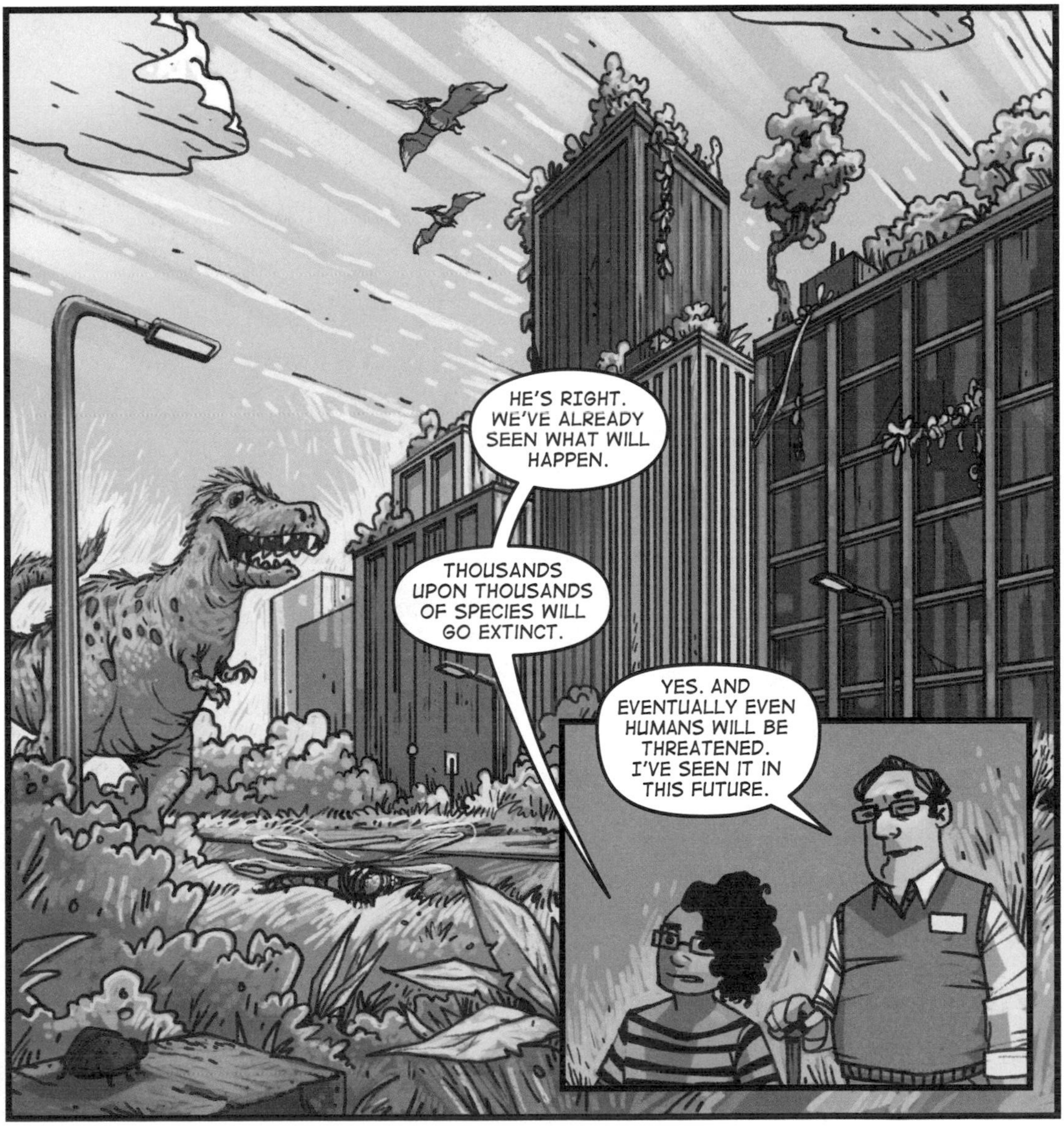
HE'S RIGHT. WE'VE ALREADY SEEN WHAT WILL HAPPEN.
THOUSANDS UPON THOUSANDS OF SPECIES WILL GO EXTINCT.
YES. AND EVENTUALLY EVEN HUMANS WILL BE THREATENED. I'VE SEEN IT IN THIS FUTURE.

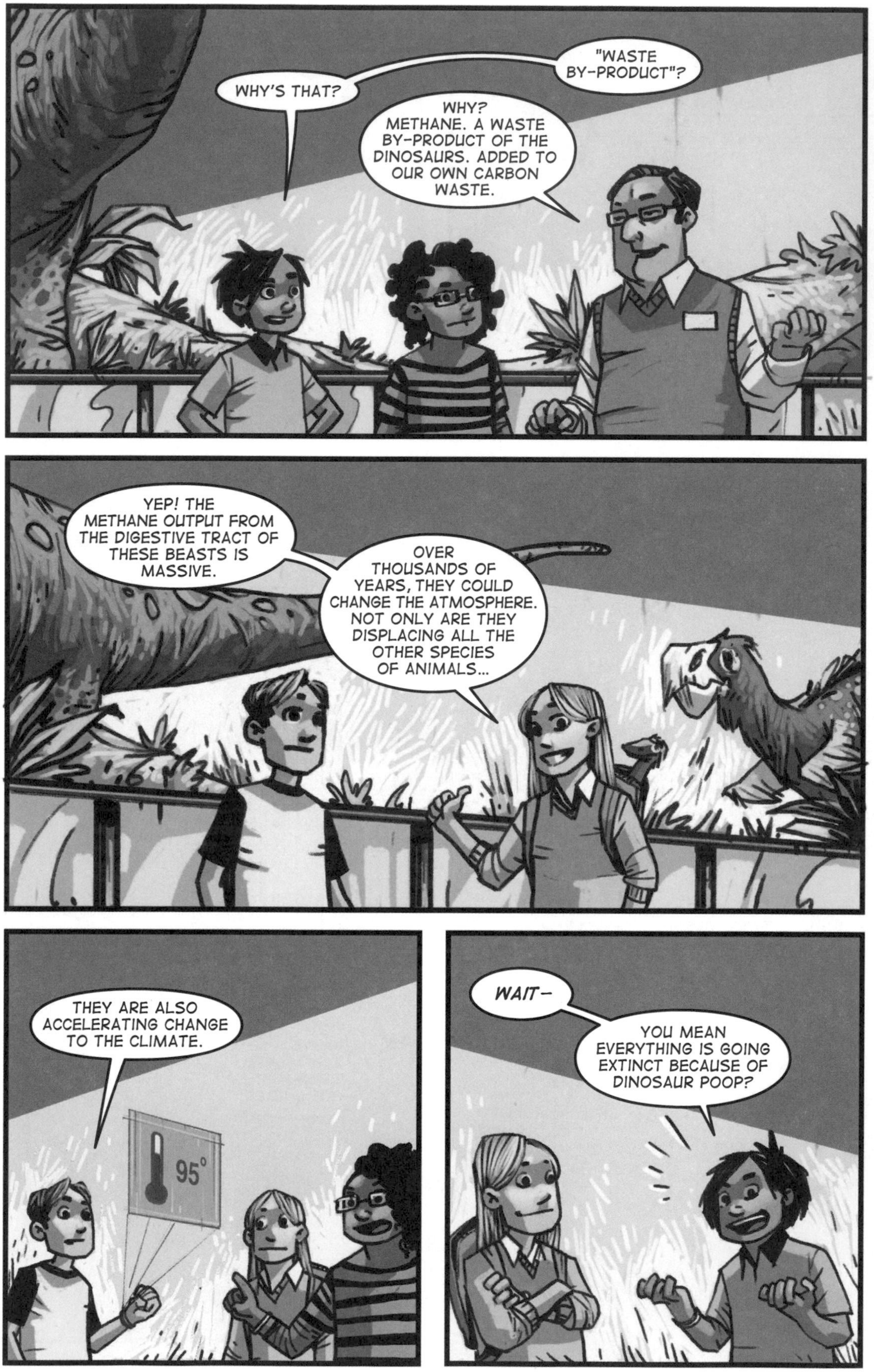
WHY'S THAT?
"WASTE BY-PRODUCT"?
WHY? METHANE. A WASTE BY-PRODUCT OF THE DINOSAURS. ADDED TO OUR OWN CARBON WASTE.
YEP! THE METHANE OUTPUT FROM THE DIGESTIVE TRACT OF THESE BEASTS IS MASSIVE.
OVER THOUSANDS OF YEARS, THEY COULD CHANGE THE ATMOSPHERE. NOT ONLY ARE THEY DISPLACING ALL THE OTHER SPECIES OF ANIMALS...
THEY ARE ALSO ACCELERATING CHANGE TO THE CLIMATE.
95°
WAIT–
YOU MEAN EVERYTHING IS GOING EXTINCT BECAUSE OF DINOSAUR POOP?

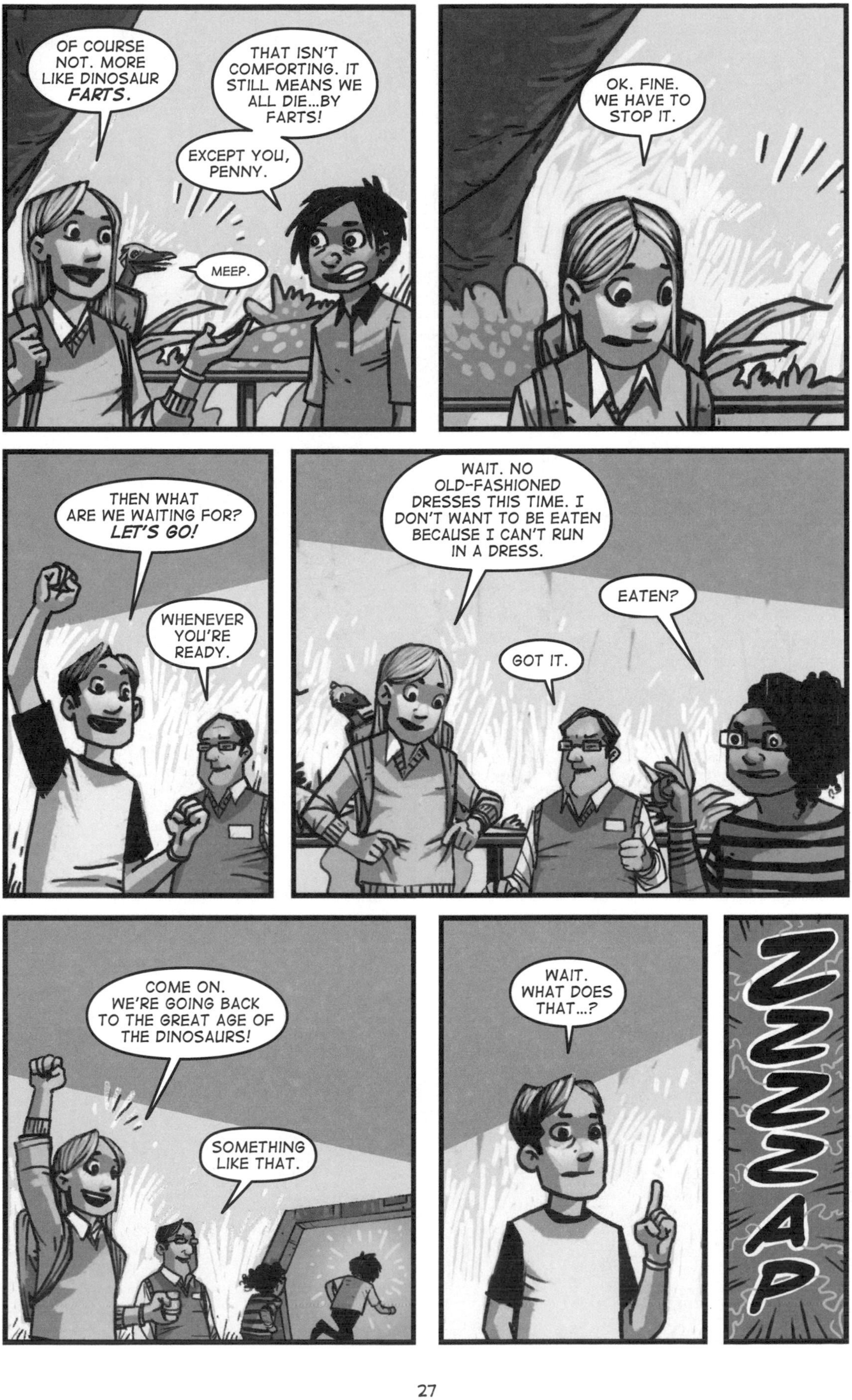

OF COURSE NOT. MORE LIKE DINOSAUR **FARTS**.
THAT ISN'T COMFORTING. IT STILL MEANS WE ALL DIE...BY FARTS!
EXCEPT YOU, PENNY.
MEEP.
OK. FINE. WE HAVE TO STOP IT.
THEN WHAT ARE WE WAITING FOR? **LET'S GO!**
WHENEVER YOU'RE READY.
WAIT. NO OLD-FASHIONED DRESSES THIS TIME. I DON'T WANT TO BE EATEN BECAUSE I CAN'T RUN IN A DRESS.
GOT IT.
EATEN?
COME ON. WE'RE GOING BACK TO THE GREAT AGE OF THE DINOSAURS!
SOMETHING LIKE THAT.
WAIT. WHAT DOES THAT...?
ZZZZAP

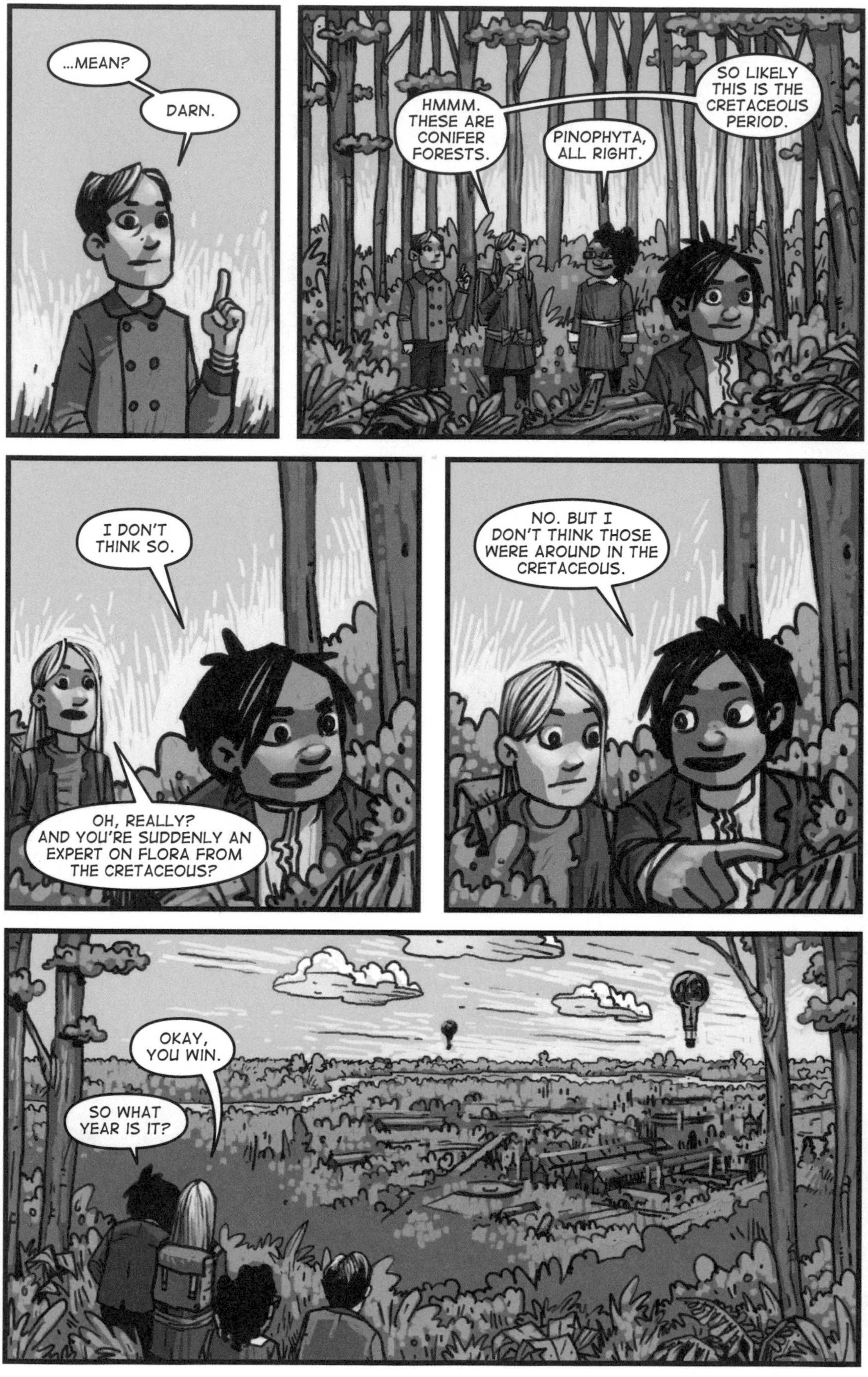
...MEAN?
DARN.
HMMM. THESE ARE CONIFER FORESTS.
PINOPHYTA, ALL RIGHT.
SO LIKELY THIS IS THE CRETACEOUS PERIOD.
I DON'T THINK SO.
OH, REALLY? AND YOU'RE SUDDENLY AN EXPERT ON FLORA FROM THE CRETACEOUS?
NO. BUT I DON'T THINK THOSE WERE AROUND IN THE CRETACEOUS.
OKAY, YOU WIN.
SO WHAT YEAR IS IT?

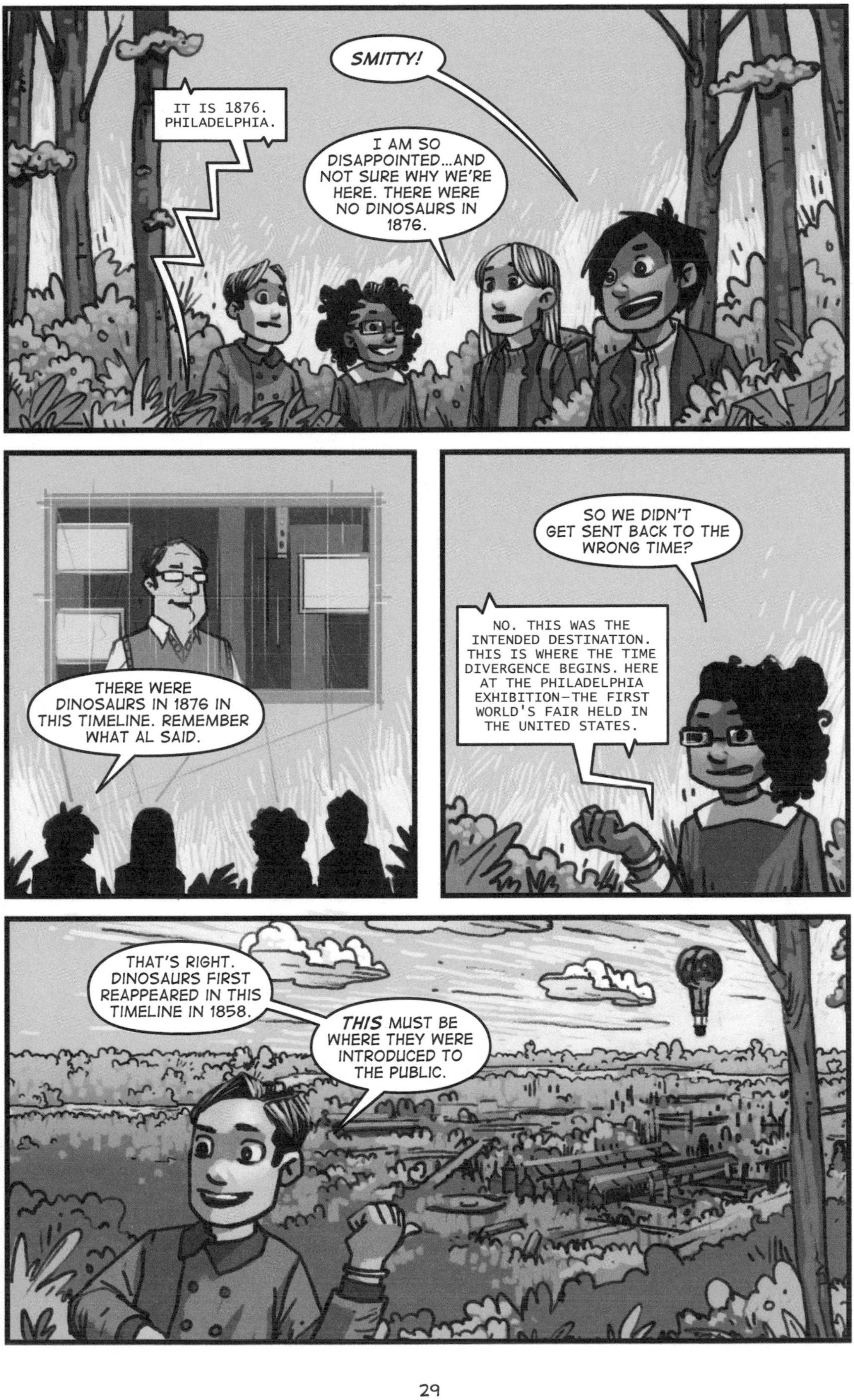
IT IS 1876. PHILADELPHIA.
SMITTY!
I AM SO DISAPPOINTED...AND NOT SURE WHY WE'RE HERE. THERE WERE NO DINOSAURS IN 1876.
THERE WERE DINOSAURS IN 1876 IN THIS TIMELINE. REMEMBER WHAT AL SAID.
SO WE DIDN'T GET SENT BACK TO THE WRONG TIME?
NO. THIS WAS THE INTENDED DESTINATION. THIS IS WHERE THE TIME DIVERGENCE BEGINS. HERE AT THE PHILADELPHIA EXHIBITION—THE FIRST WORLD'S FAIR HELD IN THE UNITED STATES.
THAT'S RIGHT. DINOSAURS FIRST REAPPEARED IN THIS TIMELINE IN 1858.
THIS MUST BE WHERE THEY WERE INTRODUCED TO THE PUBLIC.

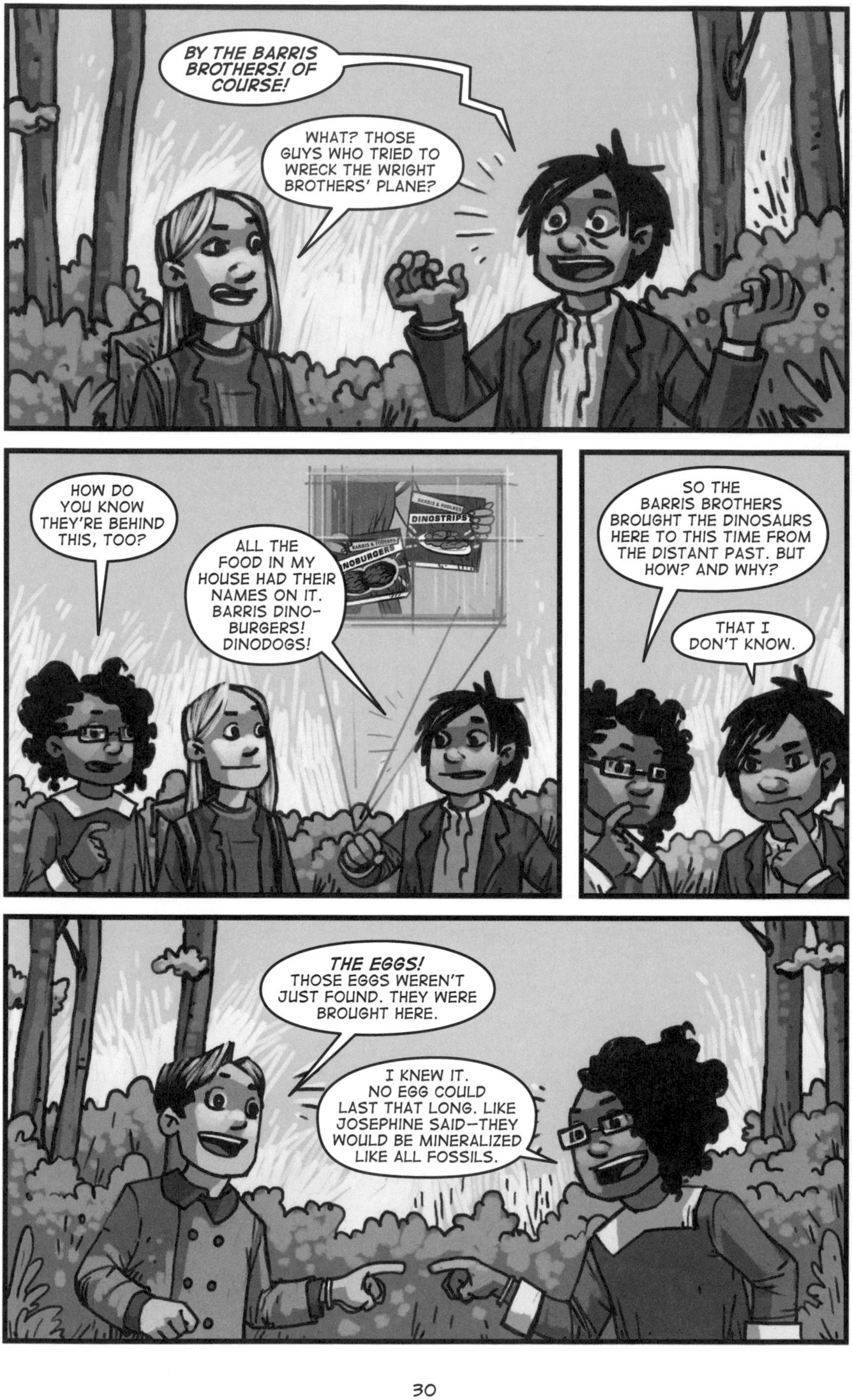

BY THE BARRIS BROTHERS! OF COURSE!
WHAT? THOSE GUYS WHO TRIED TO WRECK THE WRIGHT BROTHERS' PLANE?
HOW DO YOU KNOW THEY'RE BEHIND THIS, TOO?
ALL THE FOOD IN MY HOUSE HAD THEIR NAMES ON IT. BARRIS DINO-BURGERS! DINODOGS!
BARRIS & FOULKES
DINOSTRIPS
SO THE BARRIS BROTHERS BROUGHT THE DINOSAURS HERE TO THIS TIME FROM THE DISTANT PAST. BUT HOW? AND WHY?
THAT I DON'T KNOW.
THE EGGS! THOSE EGGS WEREN'T JUST FOUND. THEY WERE BROUGHT HERE.
I KNEW IT. NO EGG COULD LAST THAT LONG. LIKE JOSEPHINE SAID—THEY WOULD BE MINERALIZED LIKE ALL FOSSILS.

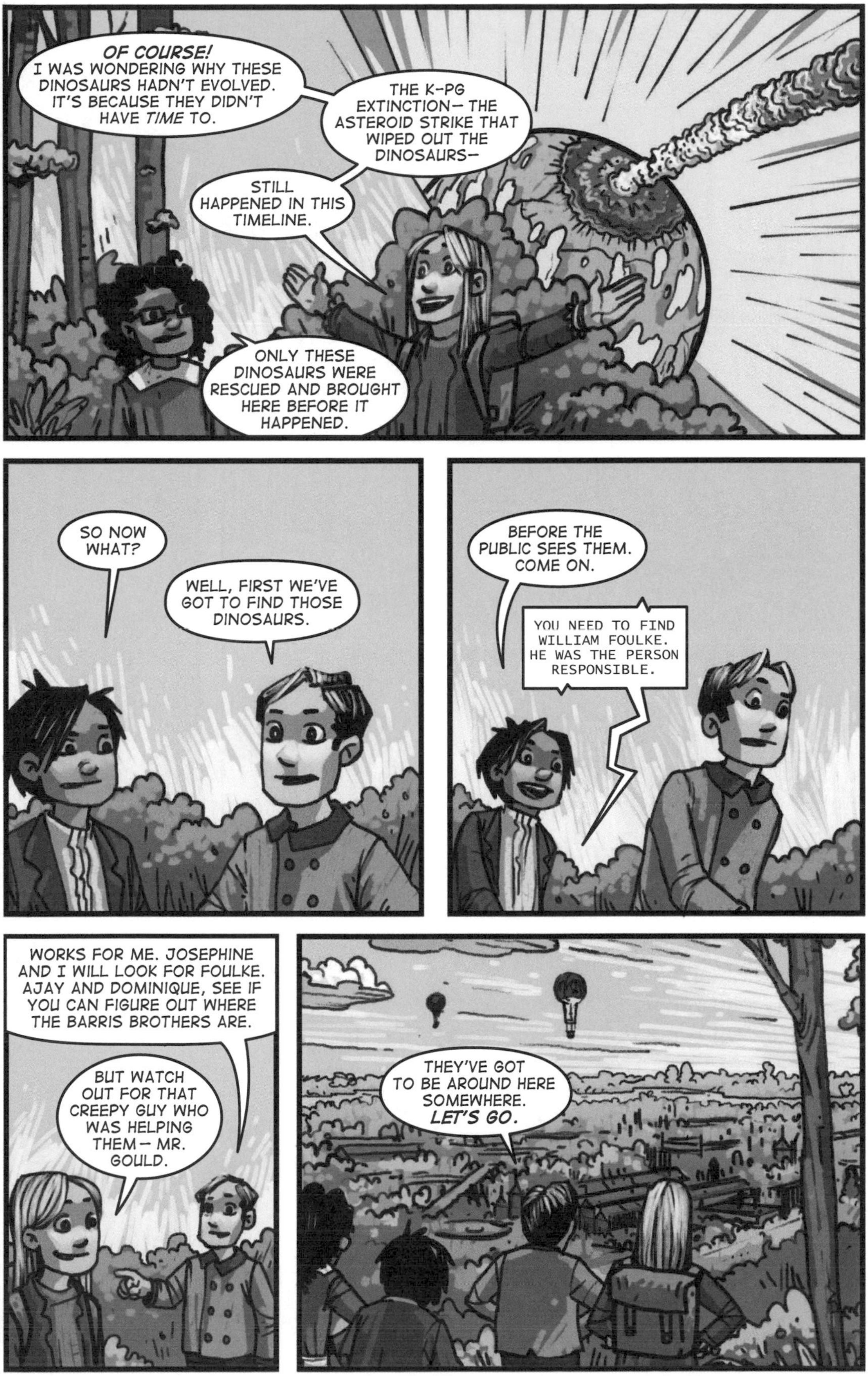
OF COURSE! I WAS WONDERING WHY THESE DINOSAURS HADN'T EVOLVED. IT'S BECAUSE THEY DIDN'T HAVE TIME TO.
THE K-PG EXTINCTION— THE ASTEROID STRIKE THAT WIPED OUT THE DINOSAURS—
STILL HAPPENED IN THIS TIMELINE.
ONLY THESE DINOSAURS WERE RESCUED AND BROUGHT HERE BEFORE IT HAPPENED.
SO NOW WHAT?
WELL, FIRST WE'VE GOT TO FIND THOSE DINOSAURS.
BEFORE THE PUBLIC SEES THEM. COME ON.
YOU NEED TO FIND WILLIAM FOULKE. HE WAS THE PERSON RESPONSIBLE.
WORKS FOR ME. JOSEPHINE AND I WILL LOOK FOR FOULKE. AJAY AND DOMINIQUE, SEE IF YOU CAN FIGURE OUT WHERE THE BARRIS BROTHERS ARE.
BUT WATCH OUT FOR THAT CREEPY GUY WHO WAS HELPING THEM— MR. GOULD.
THEY'VE GOT TO BE AROUND HERE SOMEWHERE. LET'S GO.

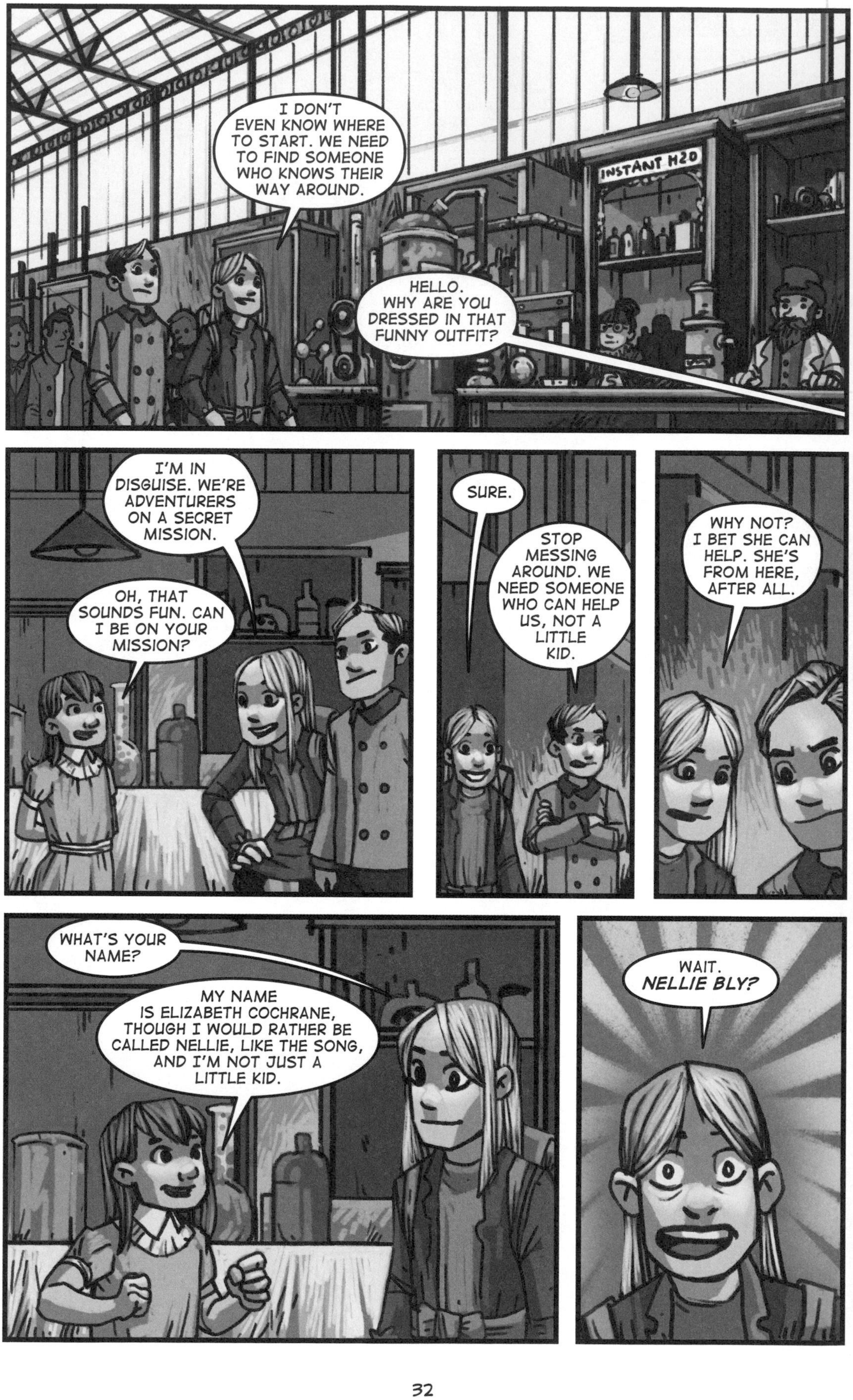
I DON'T EVEN KNOW WHERE TO START. WE NEED TO FIND SOMEONE WHO KNOWS THEIR WAY AROUND.
INSTANT H2O
HELLO. WHY ARE YOU DRESSED IN THAT FUNNY OUTFIT?
I'M IN DISGUISE. WE'RE ADVENTURERS ON A SECRET MISSION.
OH, THAT SOUNDS FUN. CAN I BE ON YOUR MISSION?
SURE.
STOP MESSING AROUND. WE NEED SOMEONE WHO CAN HELP US, NOT A LITTLE KID.
WHY NOT? I BET SHE CAN HELP. SHE'S FROM HERE, AFTER ALL.
WHAT'S YOUR NAME?
MY NAME IS ELIZABETH COCHRANE, THOUGH I WOULD RATHER BE CALLED NELLIE, LIKE THE SONG, AND I'M NOT JUST A LITTLE KID.
WAIT. *NELLIE BLY?*

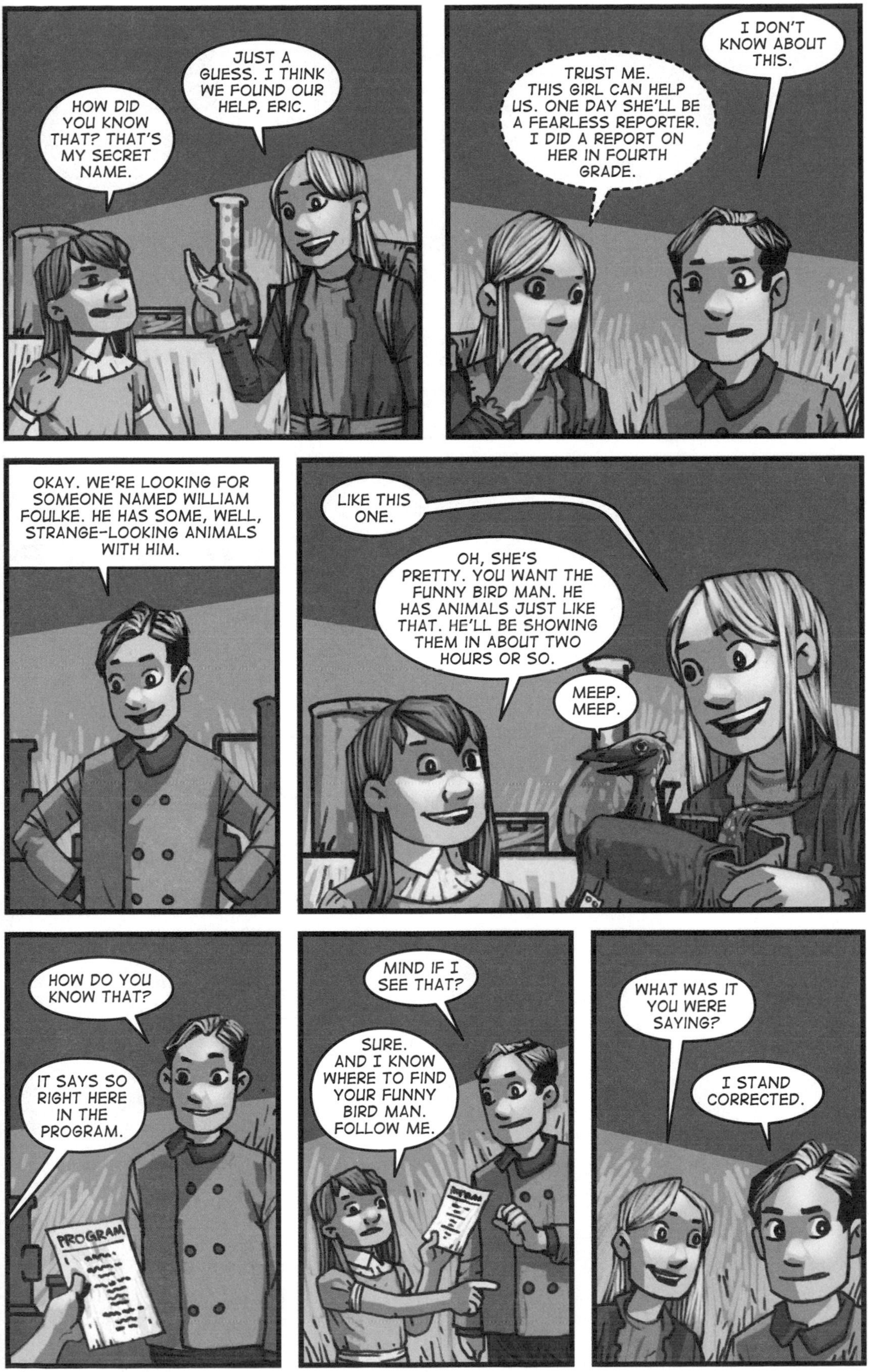
HOW DID YOU KNOW THAT? THAT'S MY SECRET NAME.
JUST A GUESS. I THINK WE FOUND OUR HELP, ERIC.
I DON'T KNOW ABOUT THIS.
TRUST ME. THIS GIRL CAN HELP US. ONE DAY SHE'LL BE A FEARLESS REPORTER. I DID A REPORT ON HER IN FOURTH GRADE.
OKAY. WE'RE LOOKING FOR SOMEONE NAMED WILLIAM FOULKE. HE HAS SOME, WELL, STRANGE-LOOKING ANIMALS WITH HIM.
LIKE THIS ONE.
OH, SHE'S PRETTY. YOU WANT THE FUNNY BIRD MAN. HE HAS ANIMALS JUST LIKE THAT. HE'LL BE SHOWING THEM IN ABOUT TWO HOURS OR SO.
MEEP. MEEP.
HOW DO YOU KNOW THAT?
IT SAYS SO RIGHT HERE IN THE PROGRAM.
PROGRAM
MIND IF I SEE THAT?
SURE. AND I KNOW WHERE TO FIND YOUR FUNNY BIRD MAN. FOLLOW ME.
WHAT WAS IT YOU WERE SAYING?
I STAND CORRECTED.

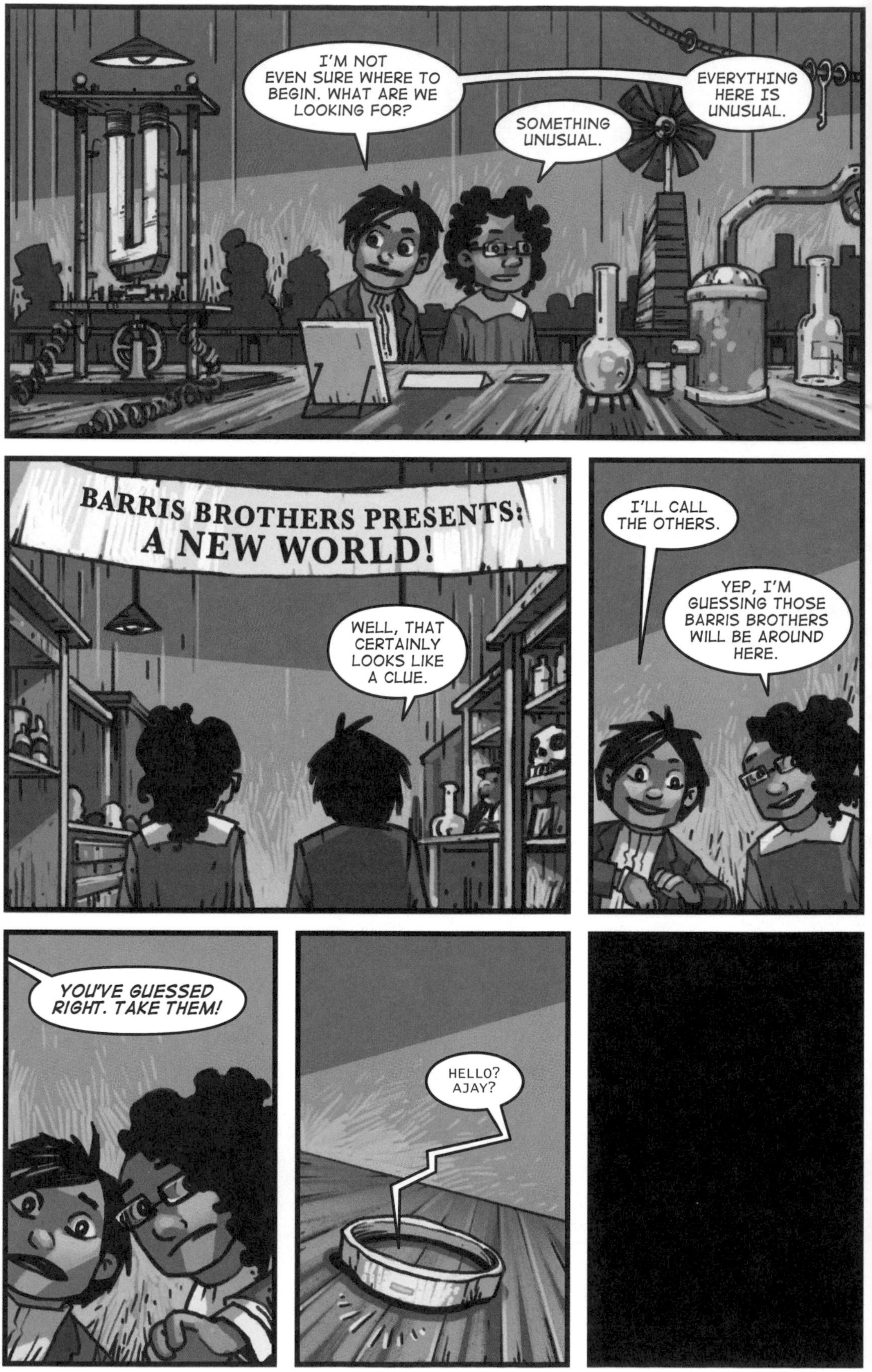

I'M NOT EVEN SURE WHERE TO BEGIN. WHAT ARE WE LOOKING FOR?
SOMETHING UNUSUAL.
EVERYTHING HERE IS UNUSUAL.
BARRIS BROTHERS PRESENTS: A NEW WORLD!
WELL, THAT CERTAINLY LOOKS LIKE A CLUE.
I'LL CALL THE OTHERS.
YEP, I'M GUESSING THOSE BARRIS BROTHERS WILL BE AROUND HERE.
YOU'VE GUESSED RIGHT. TAKE THEM!
HELLO? AJAY?

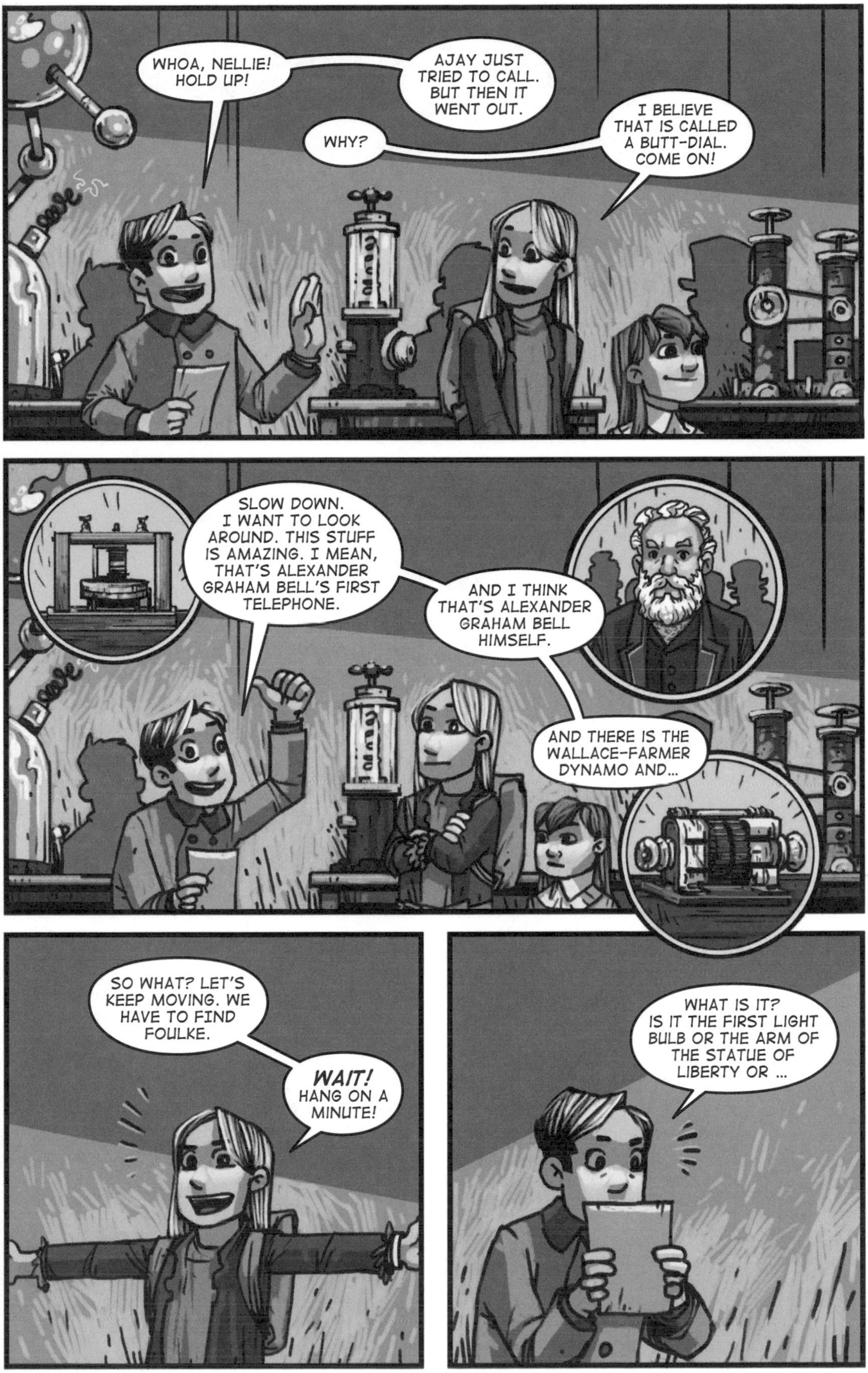
WHOA, NELLIE! HOLD UP!
AJAY JUST TRIED TO CALL. BUT THEN IT WENT OUT.
WHY?
I BELIEVE THAT IS CALLED A BUTT-DIAL. COME ON!
SLOW DOWN. I WANT TO LOOK AROUND. THIS STUFF IS AMAZING. I MEAN, THAT'S ALEXANDER GRAHAM BELL'S FIRST TELEPHONE.
AND I THINK THAT'S ALEXANDER GRAHAM BELL HIMSELF.
AND THERE IS THE WALLACE-FARMER DYNAMO AND...
SO WHAT? LET'S KEEP MOVING. WE HAVE TO FIND FOULKE.
WAIT! HANG ON A MINUTE!
WHAT IS IT? IS IT THE FIRST LIGHT BULB OR THE ARM OF THE STATUE OF LIBERTY OR ...

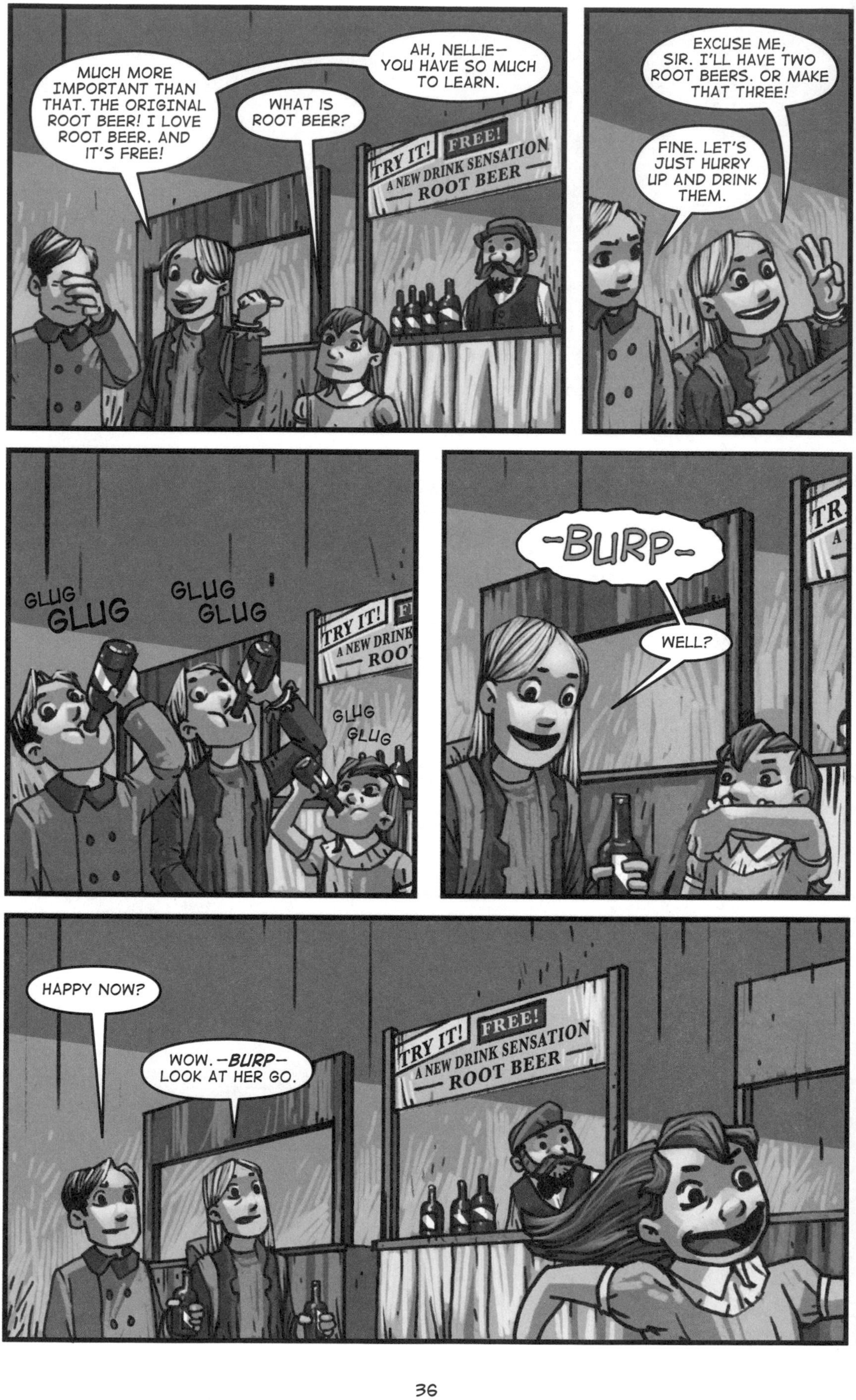

MUCH MORE IMPORTANT THAN THAT. THE ORIGINAL ROOT BEER! I LOVE ROOT BEER. AND IT'S FREE!
WHAT IS ROOT BEER?
AH, NELLIE— YOU HAVE SO MUCH TO LEARN.
TRY IT! FREE! A NEW DRINK SENSATION — ROOT BEER —
EXCUSE ME, SIR. I'LL HAVE TWO ROOT BEERS. OR MAKE THAT THREE!
FINE. LET'S JUST HURRY UP AND DRINK THEM.
GLUG GLUG
GLUG GLUG
GLUG GLUG
-BURP-
WELL?
HAPPY NOW?
WOW. —BURP— LOOK AT HER GO.
TRY IT! FREE! A NEW DRINK SENSATION — ROOT BEER —

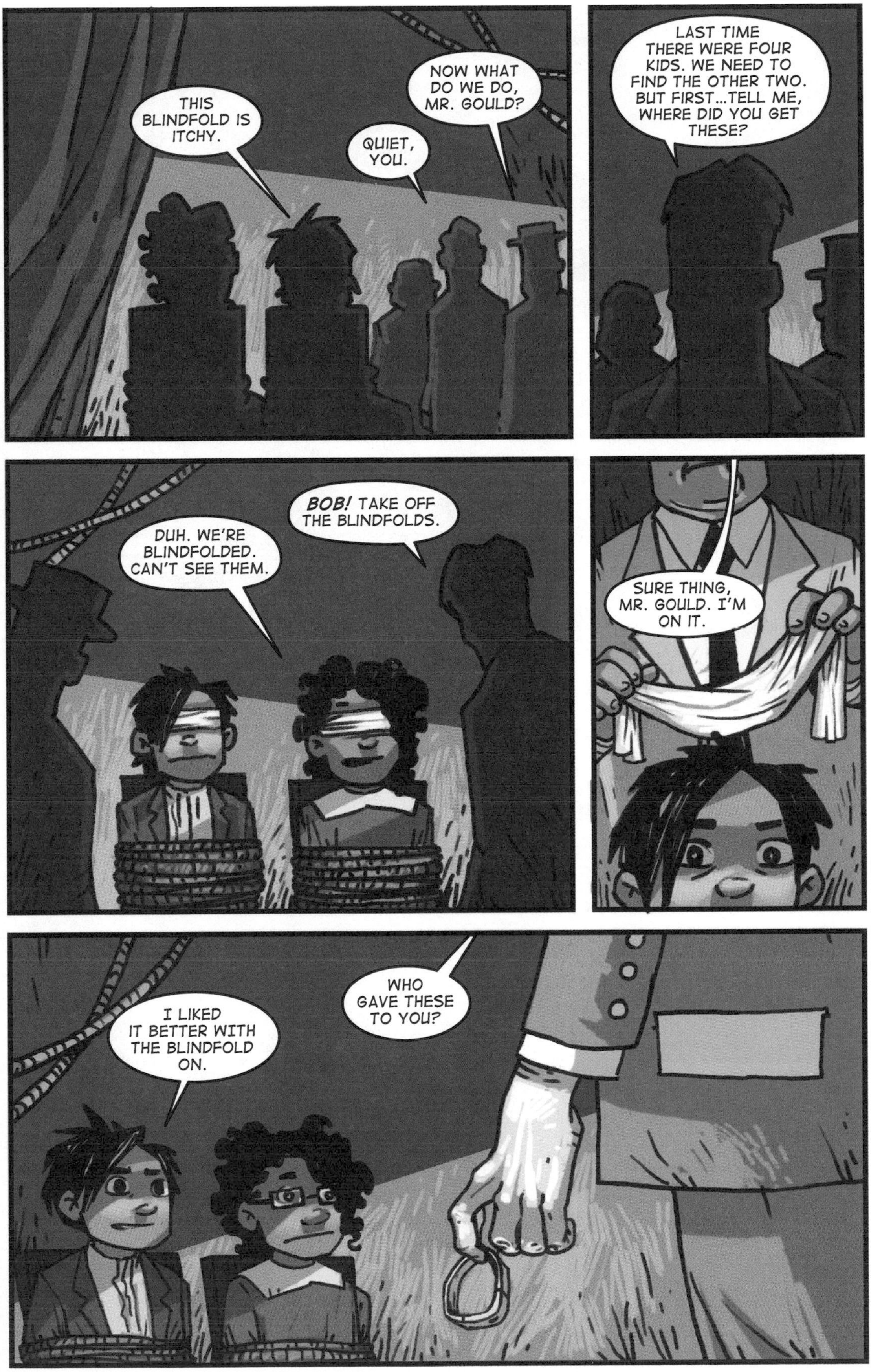
THIS BLINDFOLD IS ITCHY.
NOW WHAT DO WE DO, MR. GOULD?
QUIET, YOU.
LAST TIME THERE WERE FOUR KIDS. WE NEED TO FIND THE OTHER TWO. BUT FIRST...TELL ME, WHERE DID YOU GET THESE?
DUH. WE'RE BLINDFOLDED. CAN'T SEE THEM.
BOB! TAKE OFF THE BLINDFOLDS.
SURE THING, MR. GOULD. I'M ON IT.
I LIKED IT BETTER WITH THE BLINDFOLD ON.
WHO GAVE THESE TO YOU?

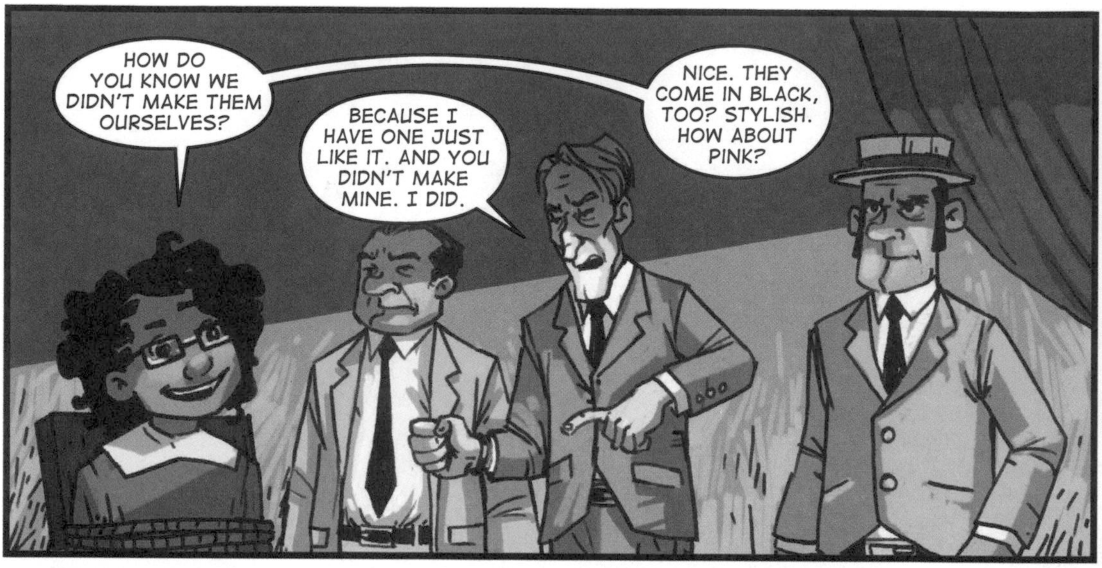
HOW DO YOU KNOW WE DIDN'T MAKE THEM OURSELVES?
BECAUSE I HAVE ONE JUST LIKE IT. AND YOU DIDN'T MAKE MINE. I DID.
NICE. THEY COME IN BLACK, TOO? STYLISH. HOW ABOUT PINK?

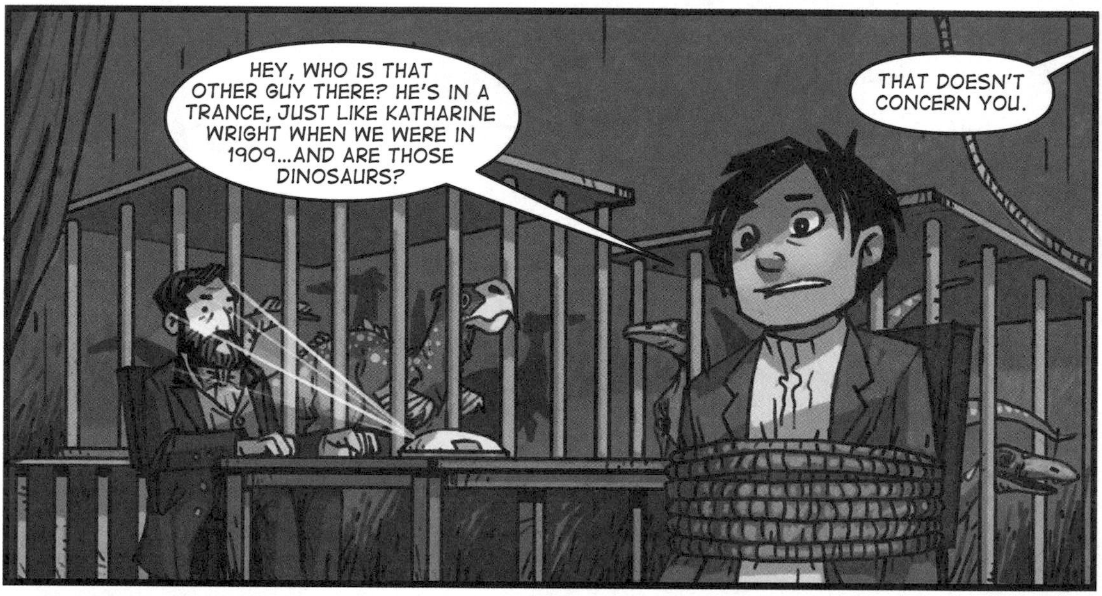
HEY, WHO IS THAT OTHER GUY THERE? HE'S IN A TRANCE, JUST LIKE KATHARINE WRIGHT WHEN WE WERE IN 1909...AND ARE THOSE DINOSAURS?
THAT DOESN'T CONCERN YOU.

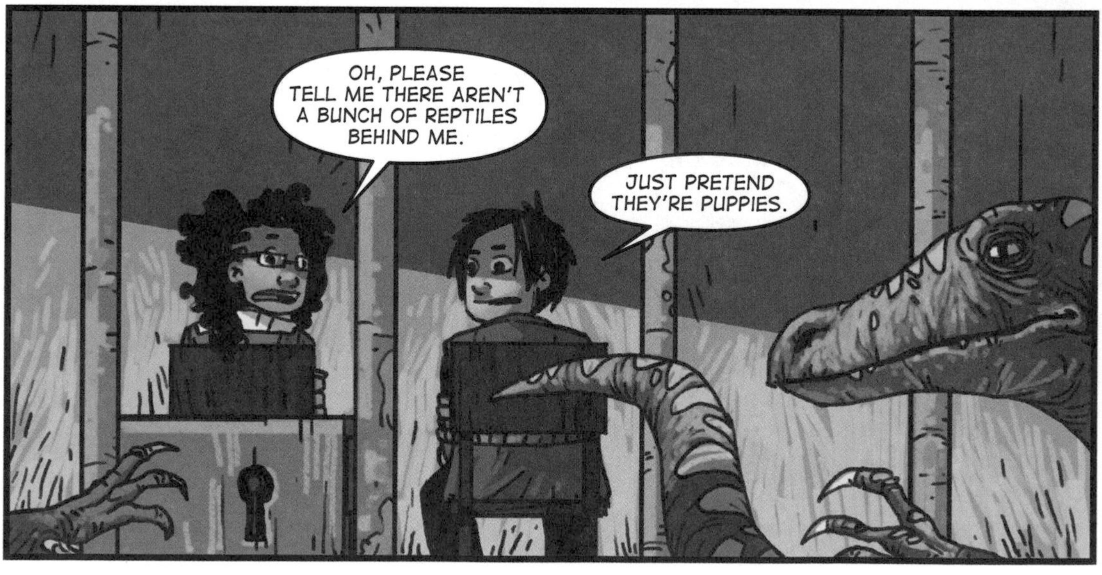
OH, PLEASE TELL ME THERE AREN'T A BUNCH OF REPTILES BEHIND ME.
JUST PRETEND THEY'RE PUPPIES.

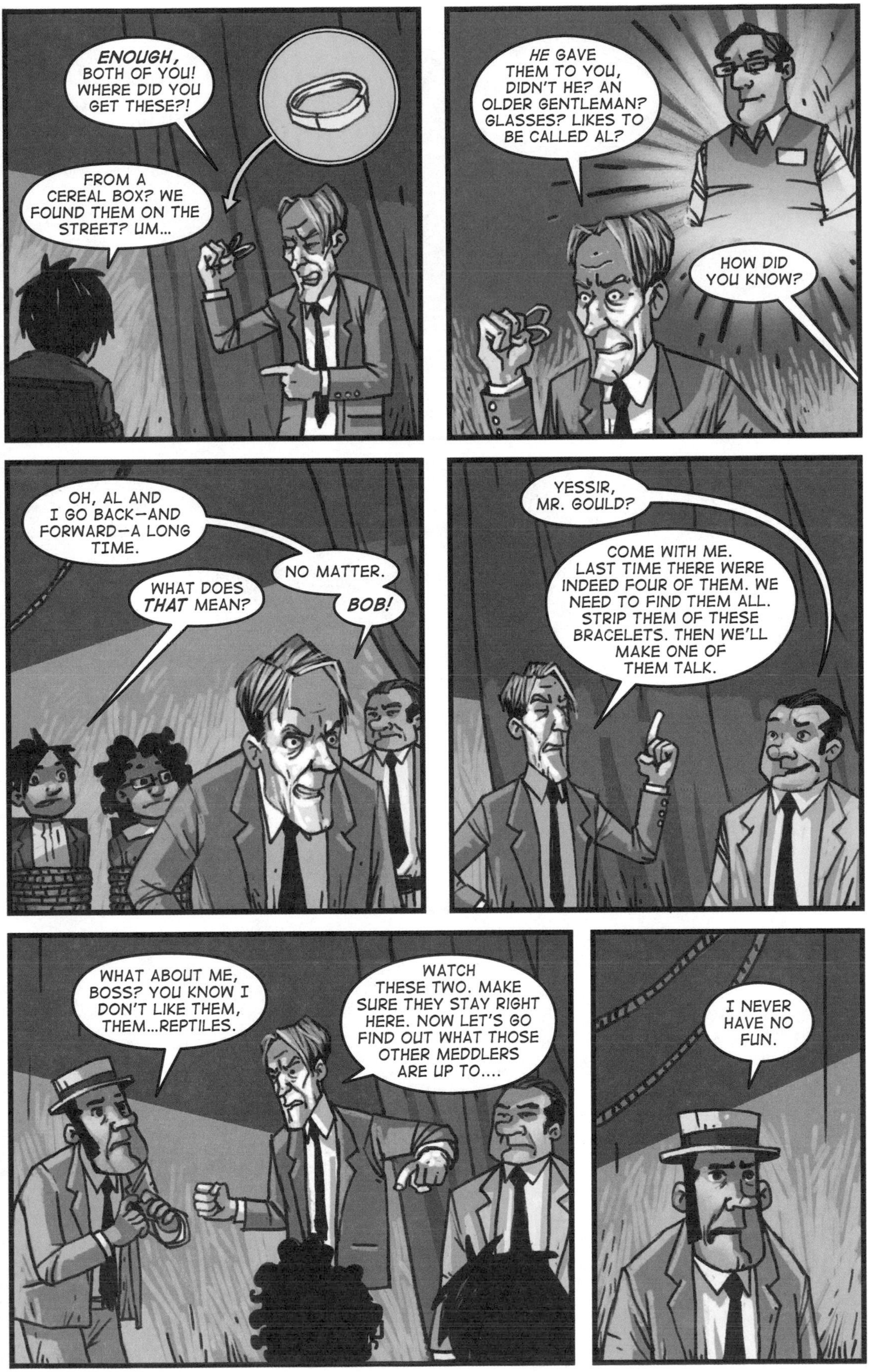
ENOUGH, BOTH OF YOU! WHERE DID YOU GET THESE?!
FROM A CEREAL BOX? WE FOUND THEM ON THE STREET? UM...
HE GAVE THEM TO YOU, DIDN'T HE? AN OLDER GENTLEMAN? GLASSES? LIKES TO BE CALLED AL?
HOW DID YOU KNOW?
OH, AL AND I GO BACK—AND FORWARD—A LONG TIME.
WHAT DOES THAT MEAN?
NO MATTER.
BOB!
YESSIR, MR. GOULD?
COME WITH ME. LAST TIME THERE WERE INDEED FOUR OF THEM. WE NEED TO FIND THEM ALL. STRIP THEM OF THESE BRACELETS. THEN WE'LL MAKE ONE OF THEM TALK.
WHAT ABOUT ME, BOSS? YOU KNOW I DON'T LIKE THEM, THEM...REPTILES.
WATCH THESE TWO. MAKE SURE THEY STAY RIGHT HERE. NOW LET'S GO FIND OUT WHAT THOSE OTHER MEDDLERS ARE UP TO....
I NEVER HAVE NO FUN.

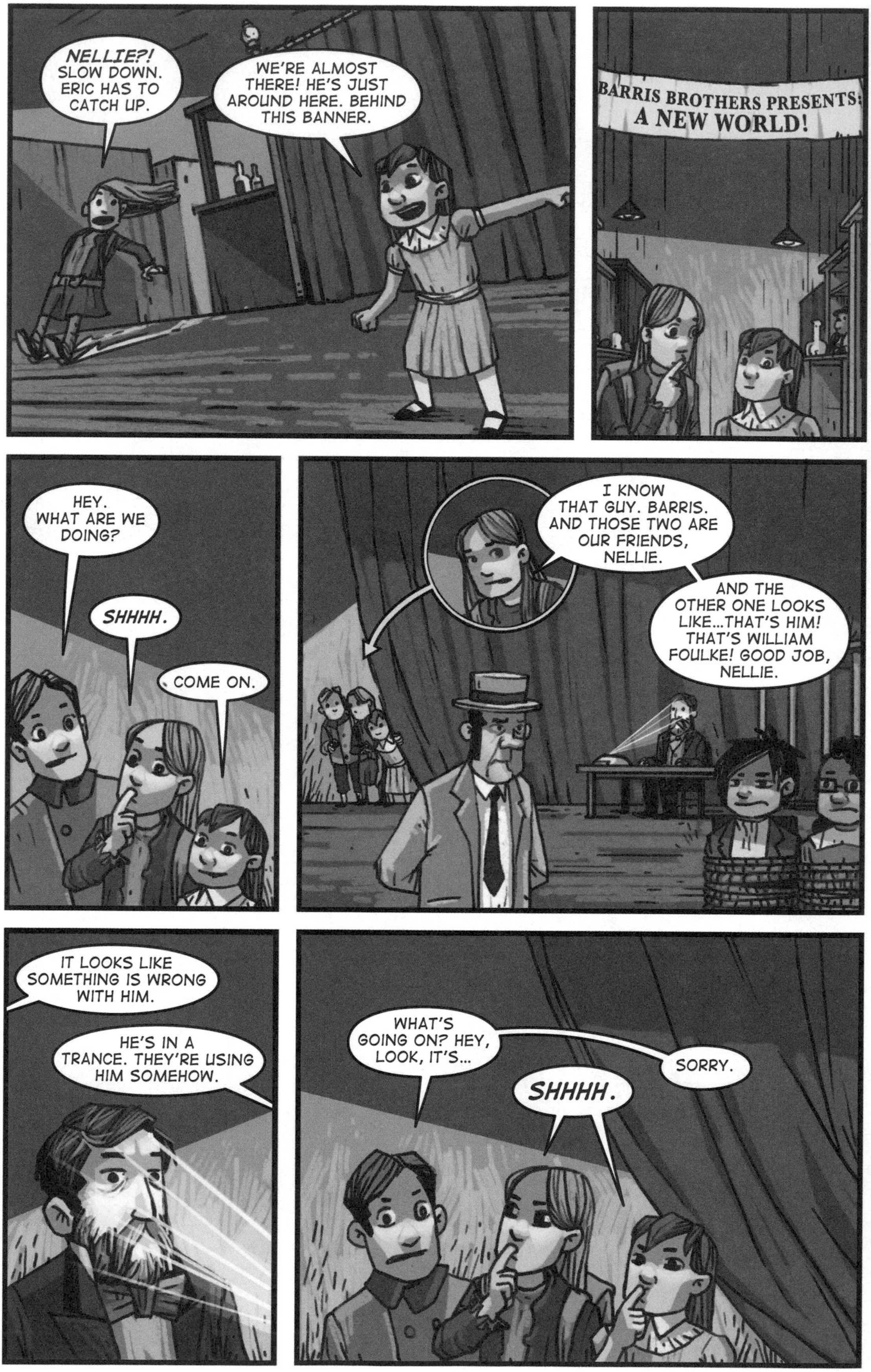
NELLIE?! SLOW DOWN. ERIC HAS TO CATCH UP.
WE'RE ALMOST THERE! HE'S JUST AROUND HERE. BEHIND THIS BANNER.
BARRIS BROTHERS PRESENTS: A NEW WORLD!
HEY. WHAT ARE WE DOING?
SHHHH.
COME ON.
I KNOW THAT GUY. BARRIS. AND THOSE TWO ARE OUR FRIENDS, NELLIE.
AND THE OTHER ONE LOOKS LIKE...THAT'S HIM! THAT'S WILLIAM FOULKE! GOOD JOB, NELLIE.
IT LOOKS LIKE SOMETHING IS WRONG WITH HIM.
HE'S IN A TRANCE. THEY'RE USING HIM SOMEHOW.
WHAT'S GOING ON? HEY, LOOK, IT'S...
SORRY.
SHHHH.

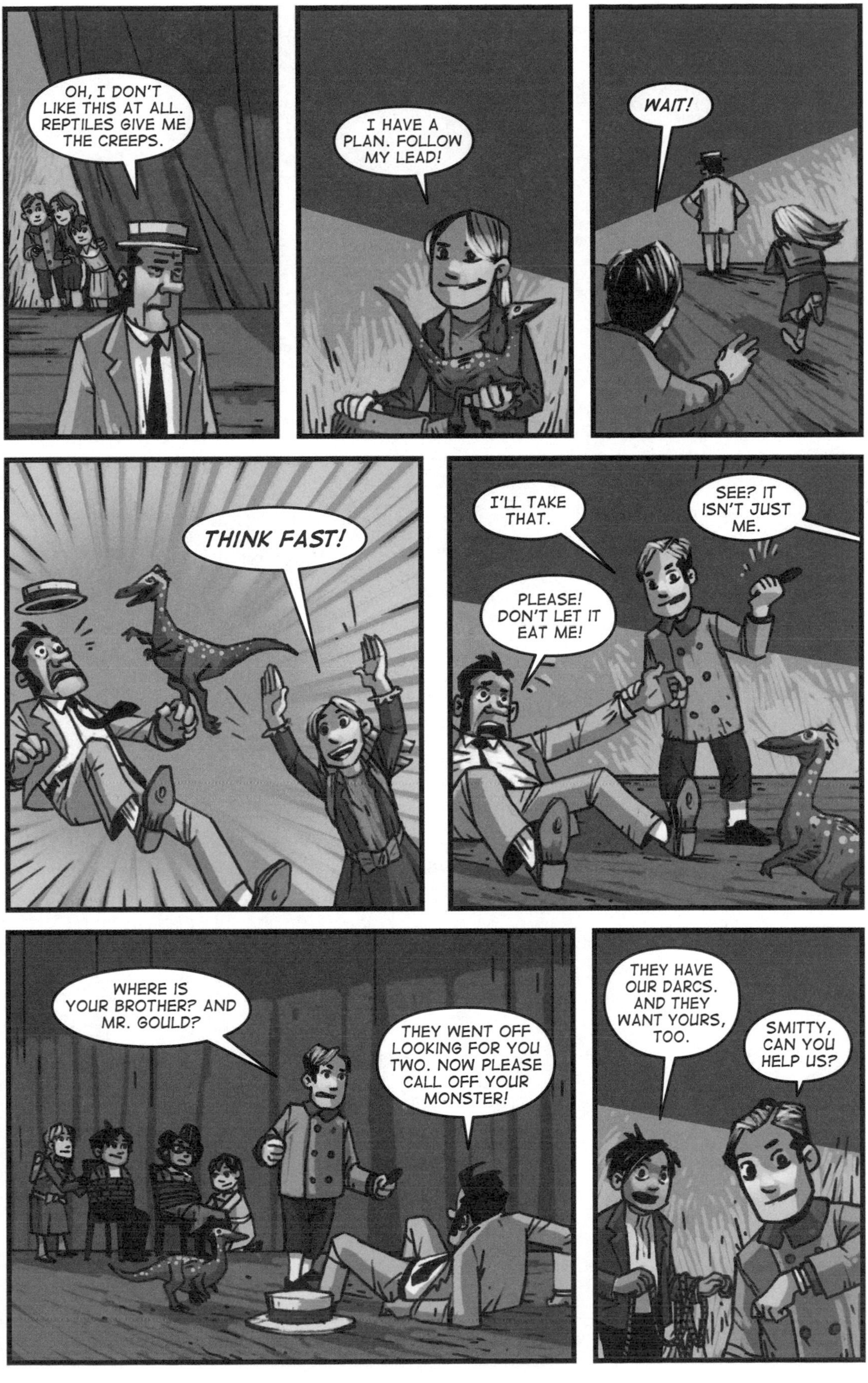
OH, I DON'T LIKE THIS AT ALL. REPTILES GIVE ME THE CREEPS.
I HAVE A PLAN. FOLLOW MY LEAD!
WAIT!
THINK FAST!
I'LL TAKE THAT.
SEE? IT ISN'T JUST ME.
PLEASE! DON'T LET IT EAT ME!
WHERE IS YOUR BROTHER? AND MR. GOULD?
THEY WENT OFF LOOKING FOR YOU TWO. NOW PLEASE CALL OFF YOUR MONSTER!
THEY HAVE OUR DARCS. AND THEY WANT YOURS, TOO.
SMITTY, CAN YOU HELP US?

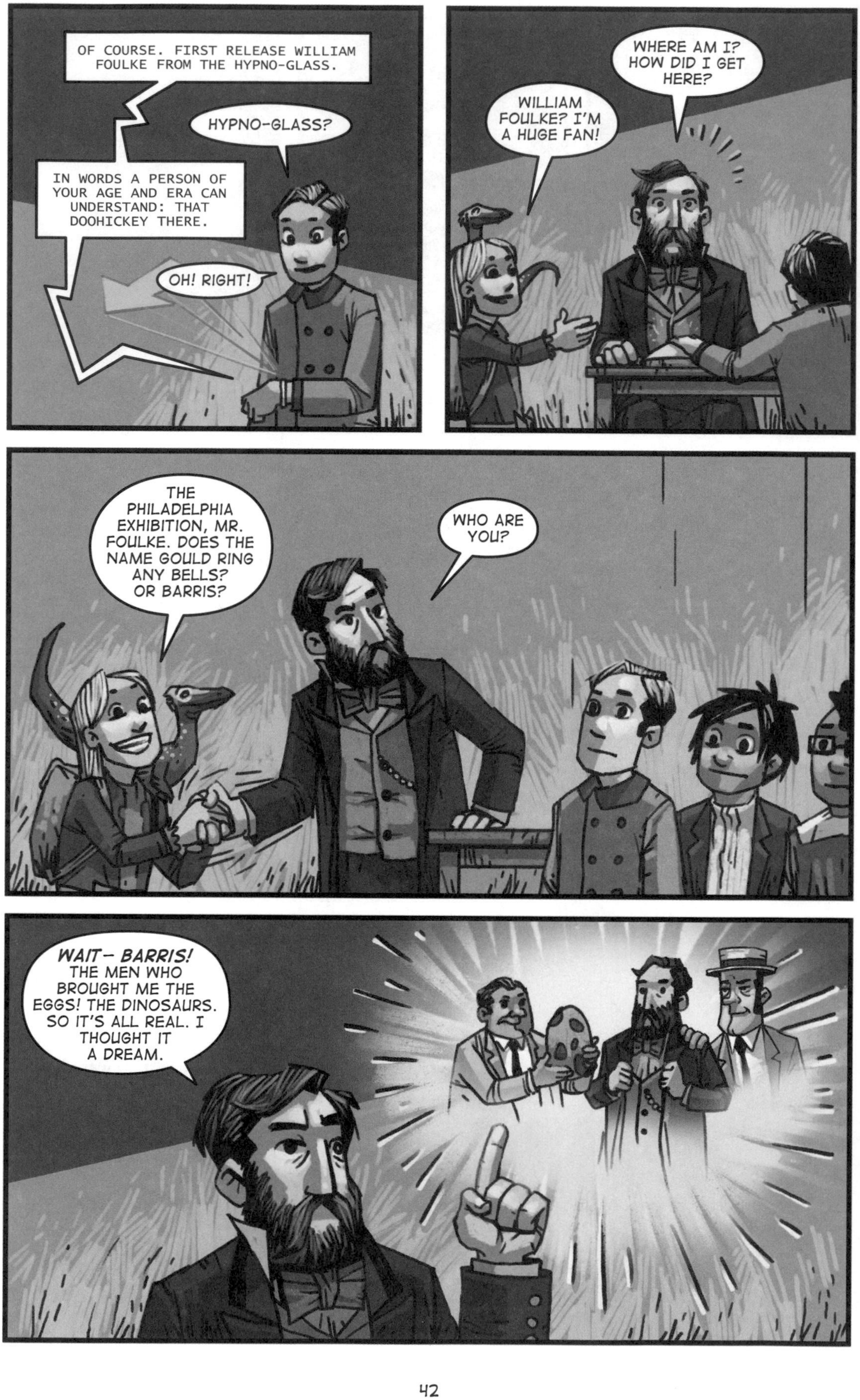
OF COURSE. FIRST RELEASE WILLIAM FOULKE FROM THE HYPNO-GLASS.
HYPNO-GLASS?
IN WORDS A PERSON OF YOUR AGE AND ERA CAN UNDERSTAND: THAT DOOHICKEY THERE.
OH! RIGHT!
WHERE AM I? HOW DID I GET HERE?
WILLIAM FOULKE? I'M A HUGE FAN!
THE PHILADELPHIA EXHIBITION, MR. FOULKE. DOES THE NAME GOULD RING ANY BELLS? OR BARRIS?
WHO ARE YOU?
WAIT– BARRIS! THE MEN WHO BROUGHT ME THE EGGS! THE DINOSAURS. SO IT'S ALL REAL. I THOUGHT IT A DREAM.

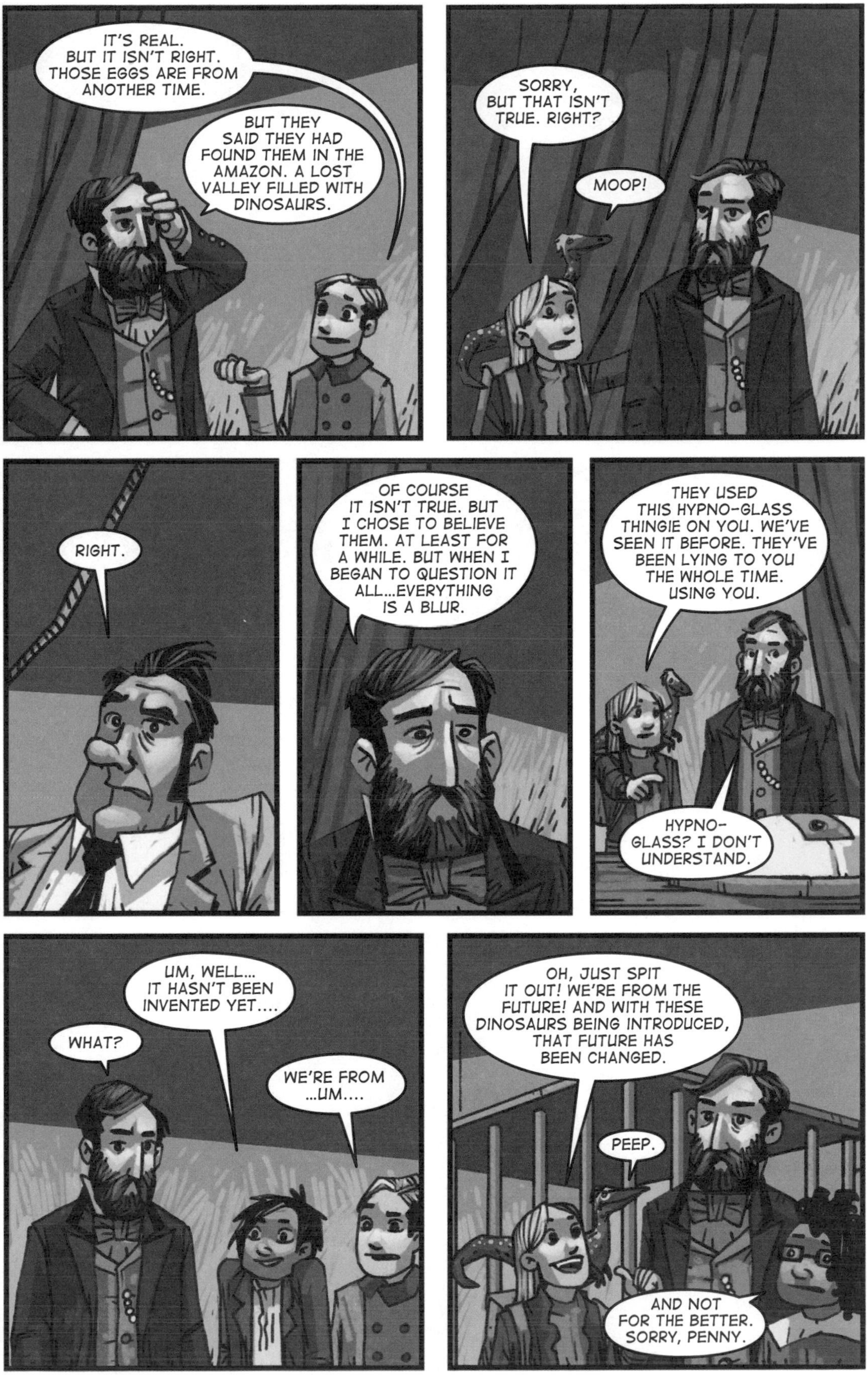
IT'S REAL. BUT IT ISN'T RIGHT. THOSE EGGS ARE FROM ANOTHER TIME.
BUT THEY SAID THEY HAD FOUND THEM IN THE AMAZON. A LOST VALLEY FILLED WITH DINOSAURS.
SORRY, BUT THAT ISN'T TRUE. RIGHT?
MOOP!
RIGHT.
OF COURSE IT ISN'T TRUE. BUT I CHOSE TO BELIEVE THEM. AT LEAST FOR A WHILE. BUT WHEN I BEGAN TO QUESTION IT ALL...EVERYTHING IS A BLUR.
THEY USED THIS HYPNO-GLASS THINGIE ON YOU. WE'VE SEEN IT BEFORE. THEY'VE BEEN LYING TO YOU THE WHOLE TIME. USING YOU.
HYPNO-GLASS? I DON'T UNDERSTAND.
WHAT?
UM, WELL... IT HASN'T BEEN INVENTED YET....
WE'RE FROM ...UM....
OH, JUST SPIT IT OUT! WE'RE FROM THE FUTURE! AND WITH THESE DINOSAURS BEING INTRODUCED, THAT FUTURE HAS BEEN CHANGED.
PEEP.
AND NOT FOR THE BETTER. SORRY, PENNY.

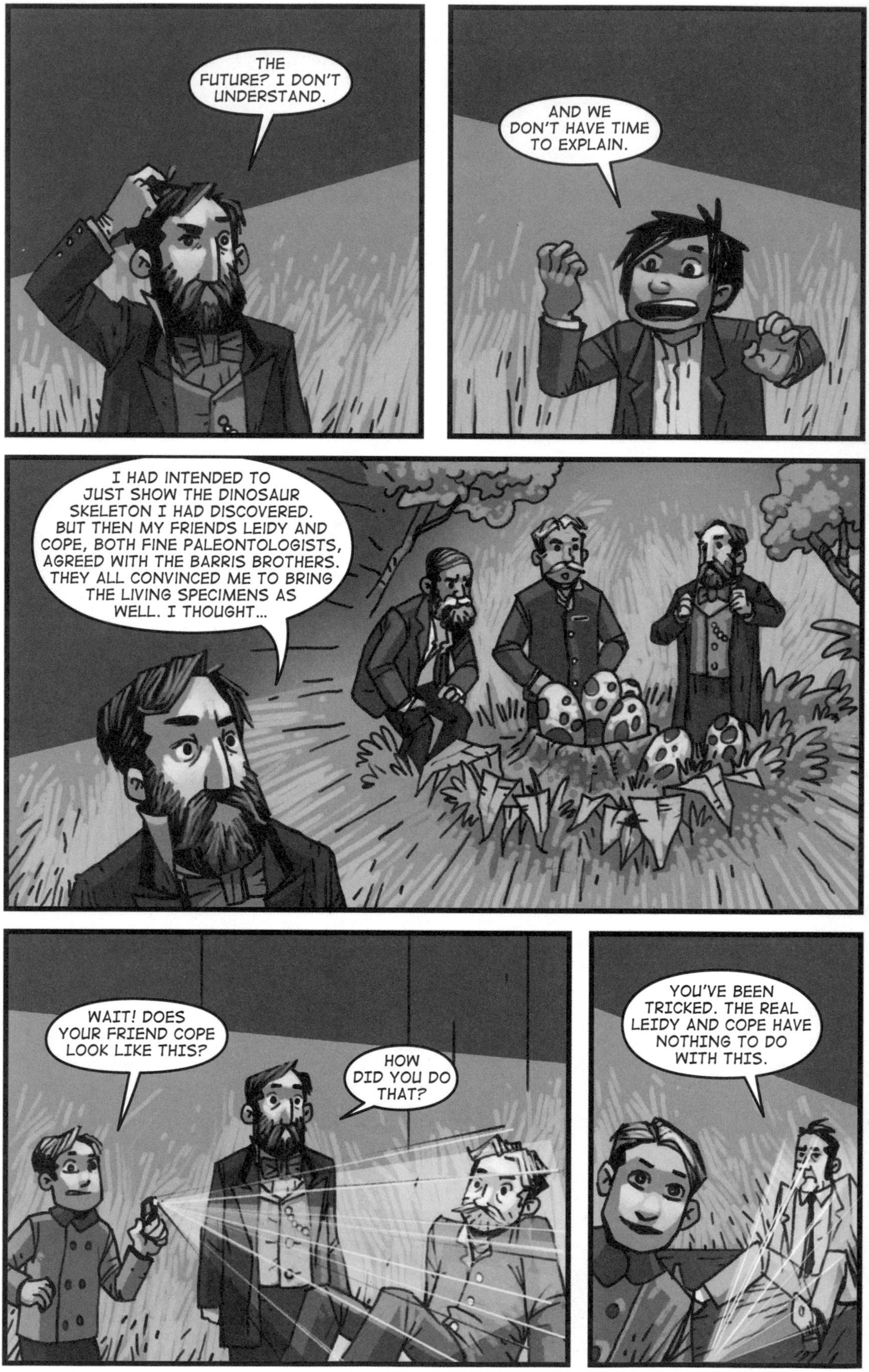
THE FUTURE? I DON'T UNDERSTAND.
AND WE DON'T HAVE TIME TO EXPLAIN.
I HAD INTENDED TO JUST SHOW THE DINOSAUR SKELETON I HAD DISCOVERED. BUT THEN MY FRIENDS LEIDY AND COPE, BOTH FINE PALEONTOLOGISTS, AGREED WITH THE BARRIS BROTHERS. THEY ALL CONVINCED ME TO BRING THE LIVING SPECIMENS AS WELL. I THOUGHT...
WAIT! DOES YOUR FRIEND COPE LOOK LIKE THIS?
HOW DID YOU DO THAT?
YOU'VE BEEN TRICKED. THE REAL LEIDY AND COPE HAVE NOTHING TO DO WITH THIS.

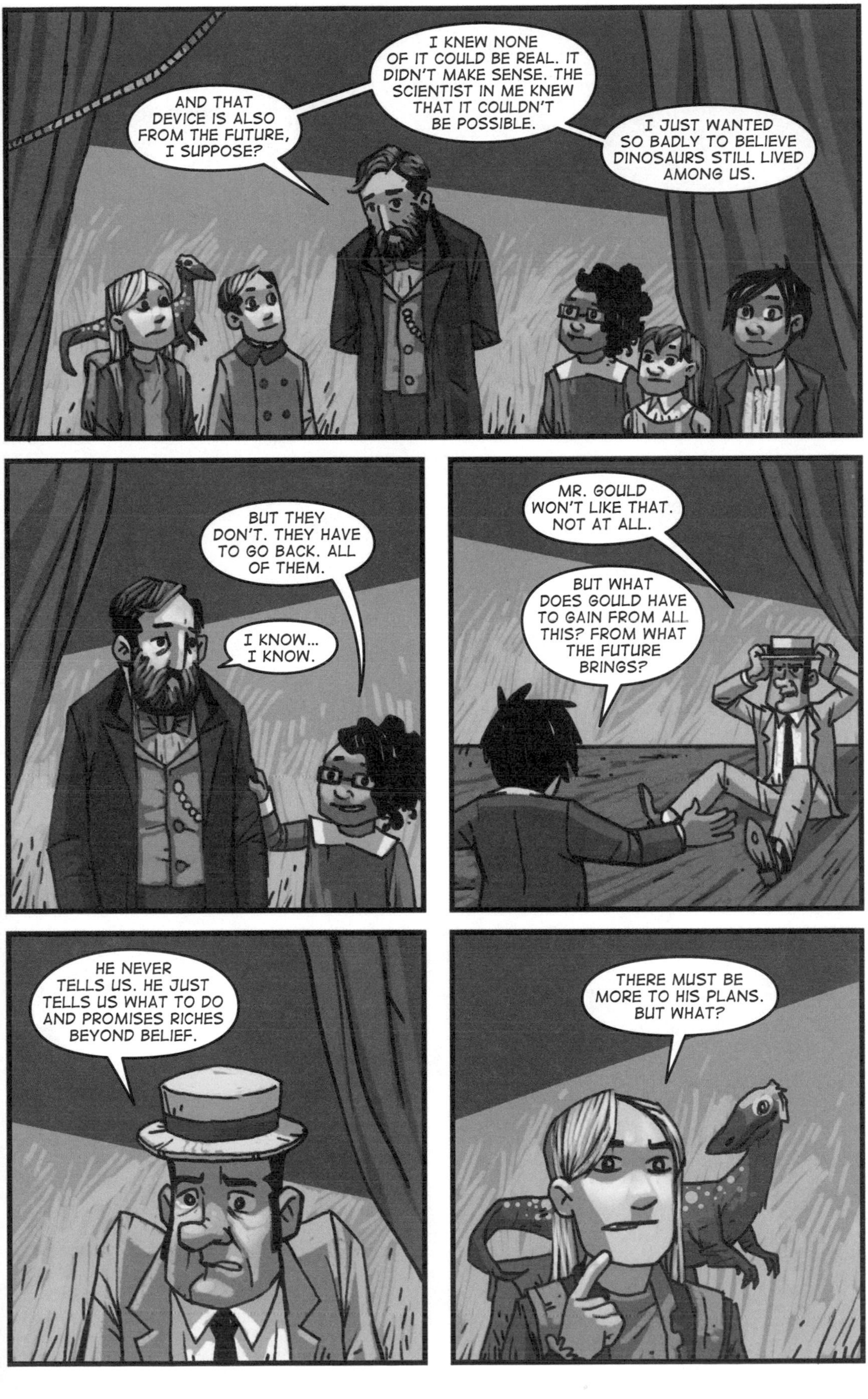
AND THAT DEVICE IS ALSO FROM THE FUTURE, I SUPPOSE?
I KNEW NONE OF IT COULD BE REAL. IT DIDN'T MAKE SENSE. THE SCIENTIST IN ME KNEW THAT IT COULDN'T BE POSSIBLE.
I JUST WANTED SO BADLY TO BELIEVE DINOSAURS STILL LIVED AMONG US.
BUT THEY DON'T. THEY HAVE TO GO BACK. ALL OF THEM.
I KNOW... I KNOW.
MR. GOULD WON'T LIKE THAT. NOT AT ALL.
BUT WHAT DOES GOULD HAVE TO GAIN FROM ALL THIS? FROM WHAT THE FUTURE BRINGS?
HE NEVER TELLS US. HE JUST TELLS US WHAT TO DO AND PROMISES RICHES BEYOND BELIEF.
THERE MUST BE MORE TO HIS PLANS. BUT WHAT?

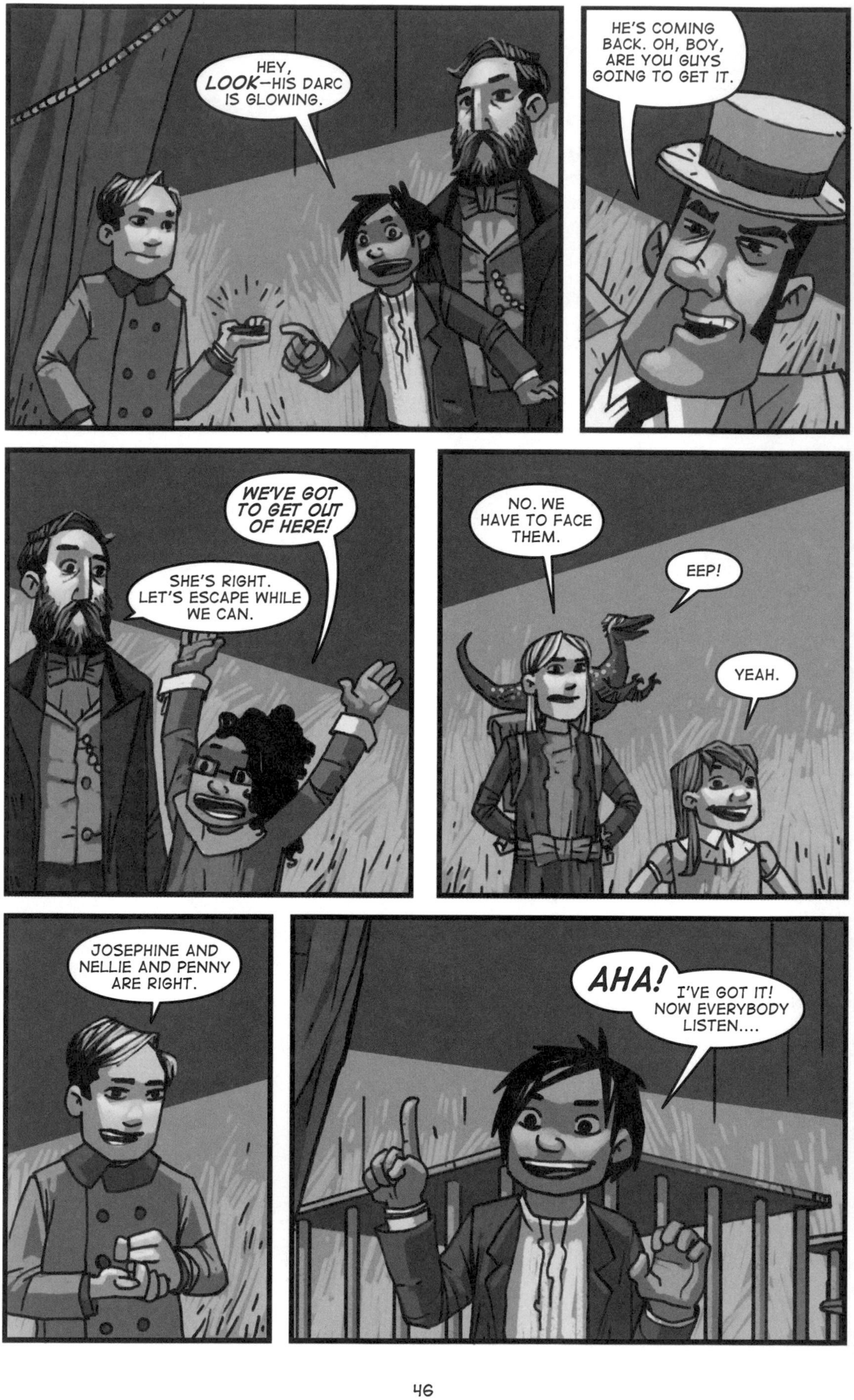
HEY, LOOK—HIS DARC IS GLOWING.
HE'S COMING BACK. OH, BOY, ARE YOU GUYS GOING TO GET IT.
WE'VE GOT TO GET OUT OF HERE!
SHE'S RIGHT. LET'S ESCAPE WHILE WE CAN.
NO. WE HAVE TO FACE THEM.
EEP!
YEAH.
JOSEPHINE AND NELLIE AND PENNY ARE RIGHT.
AHA!
I'VE GOT IT! NOW EVERYBODY LISTEN....

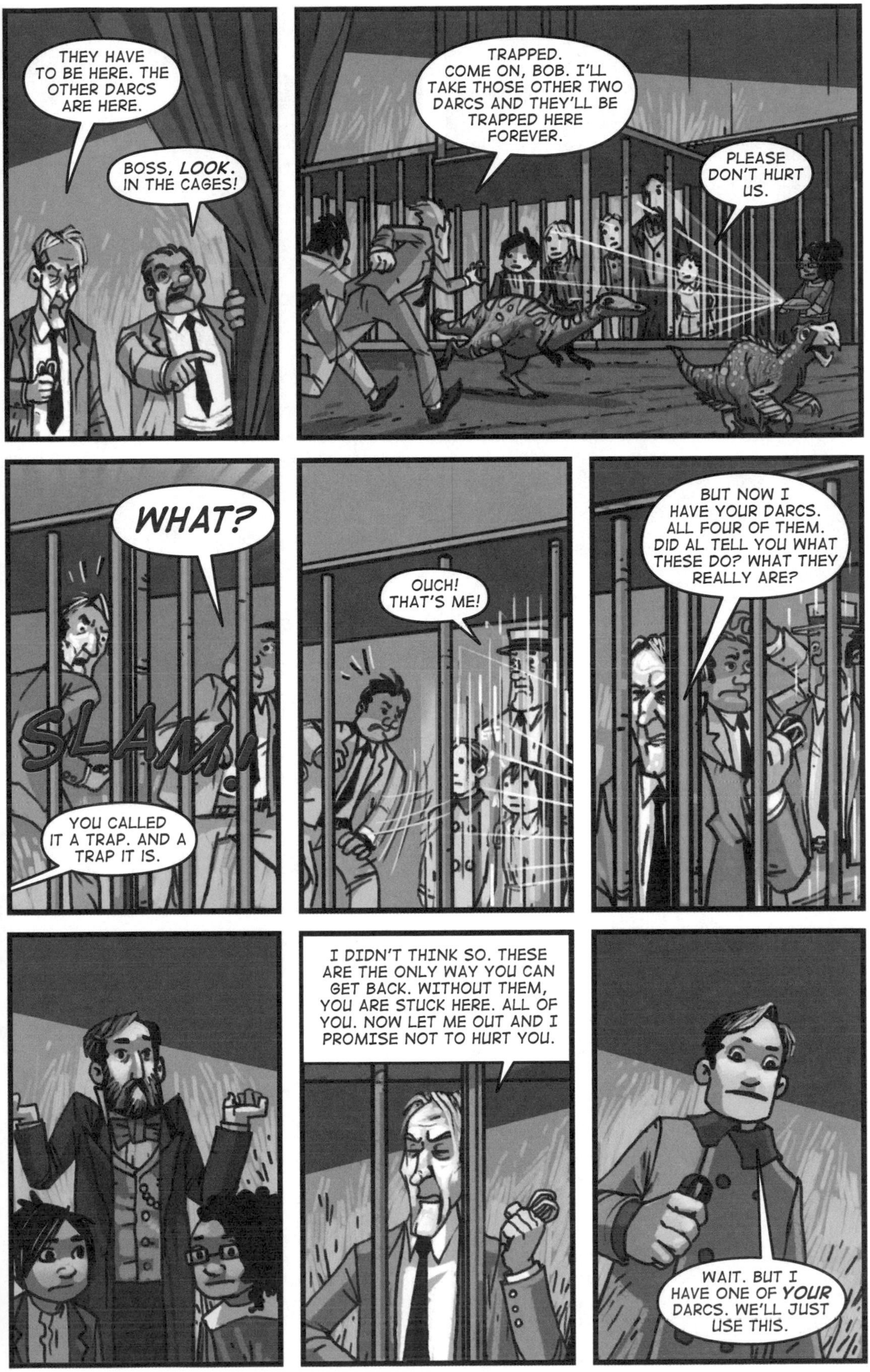
THEY HAVE TO BE HERE. THE OTHER DARCS ARE HERE.
BOSS, *LOOK.* IN THE CAGES!
TRAPPED. COME ON, BOB. I'LL TAKE THOSE OTHER TWO DARCS AND THEY'LL BE TRAPPED HERE FOREVER.
PLEASE DON'T HURT US.
WHAT?
SLAM!
YOU CALLED IT A TRAP. AND A TRAP IT IS.
OUCH! THAT'S ME!
BUT NOW I HAVE YOUR DARCS. ALL FOUR OF THEM. DID AL TELL YOU WHAT THESE DO? WHAT THEY REALLY ARE?
I DIDN'T THINK SO. THESE ARE THE ONLY WAY YOU CAN GET BACK. WITHOUT THEM, YOU ARE STUCK HERE. ALL OF YOU. NOW LET ME OUT AND I PROMISE NOT TO HURT YOU.
WAIT. BUT I HAVE ONE OF *YOUR* DARCS. WE'LL JUST USE THIS.

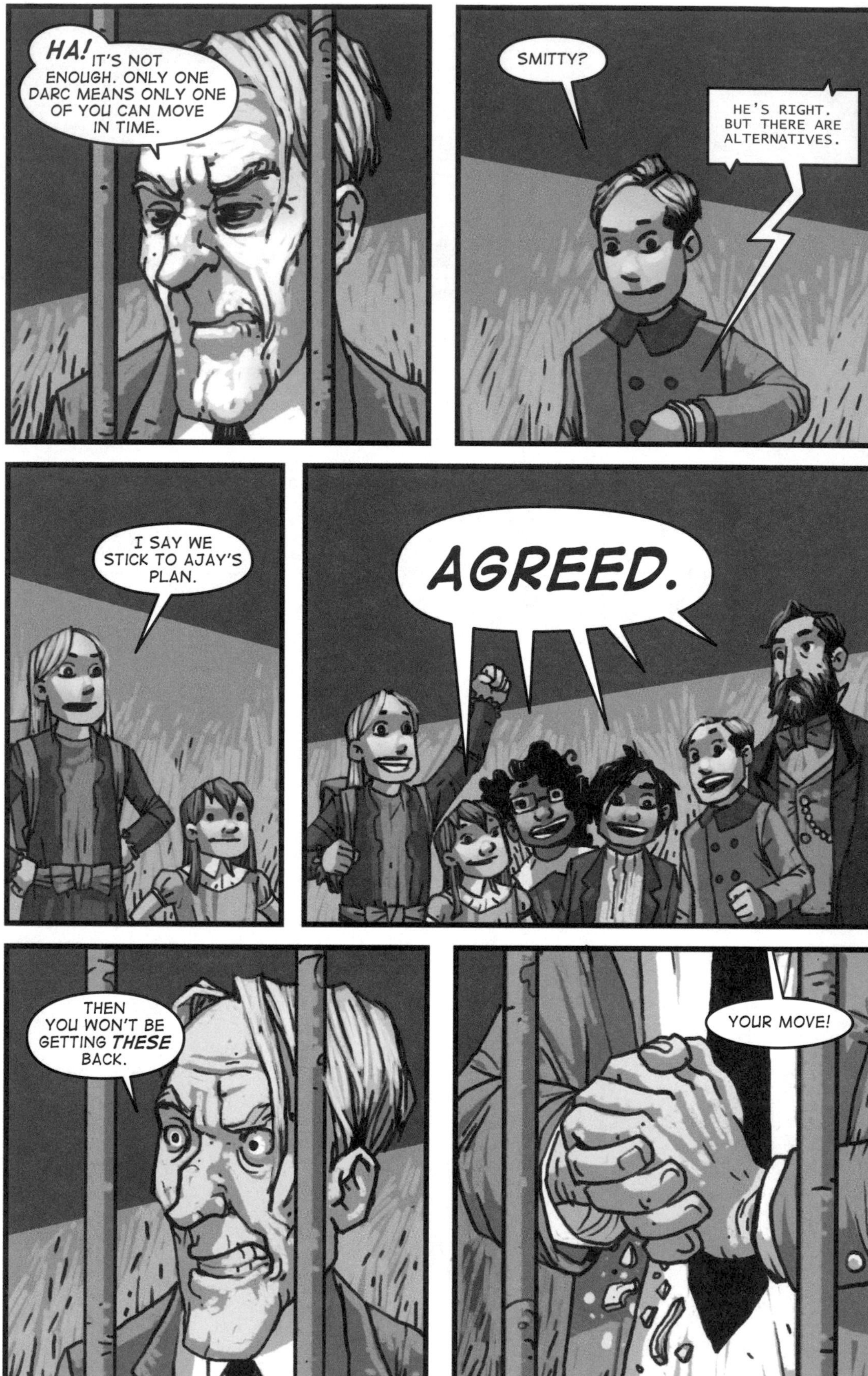
HA! IT'S NOT ENOUGH. ONLY ONE DARC MEANS ONLY ONE OF YOU CAN MOVE IN TIME.
SMITTY?
HE'S RIGHT. BUT THERE ARE ALTERNATIVES.
I SAY WE STICK TO AJAY'S PLAN.
AGREED.
THEN YOU WON'T BE GETTING *THESE* BACK.
YOUR MOVE!

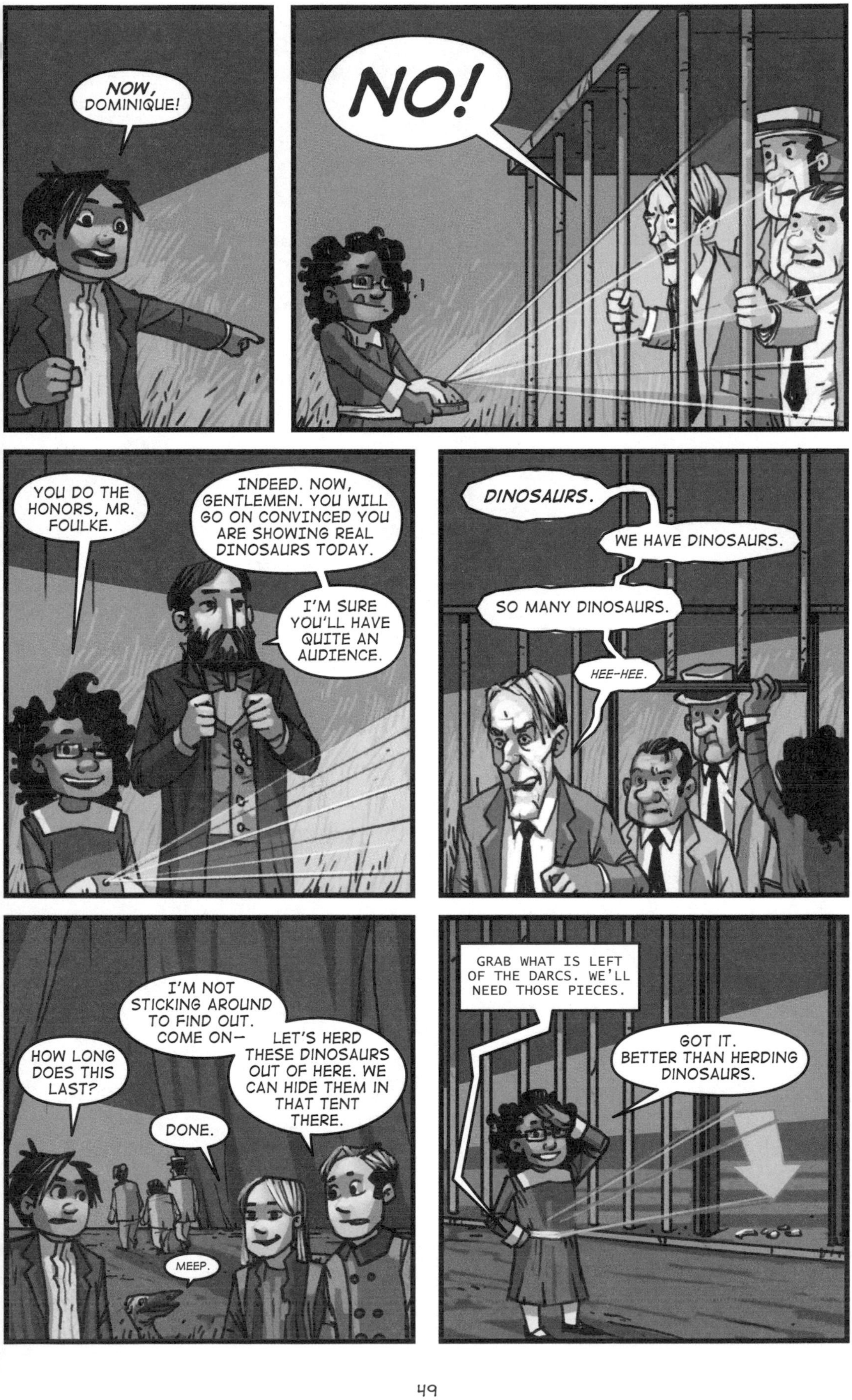
NOW, DOMINIQUE!
NO!
YOU DO THE HONORS, MR. FOULKE.
INDEED. NOW, GENTLEMEN. YOU WILL GO ON CONVINCED YOU ARE SHOWING REAL DINOSAURS TODAY.
I'M SURE YOU'LL HAVE QUITE AN AUDIENCE.
DINOSAURS.
WE HAVE DINOSAURS.
SO MANY DINOSAURS.
HEE-HEE.
HOW LONG DOES THIS LAST?
I'M NOT STICKING AROUND TO FIND OUT. COME ON—
LET'S HERD THESE DINOSAURS OUT OF HERE. WE CAN HIDE THEM IN THAT TENT THERE.
DONE.
MEEP.
GRAB WHAT IS LEFT OF THE DARCS. WE'LL NEED THOSE PIECES.
GOT IT. BETTER THAN HERDING DINOSAURS.

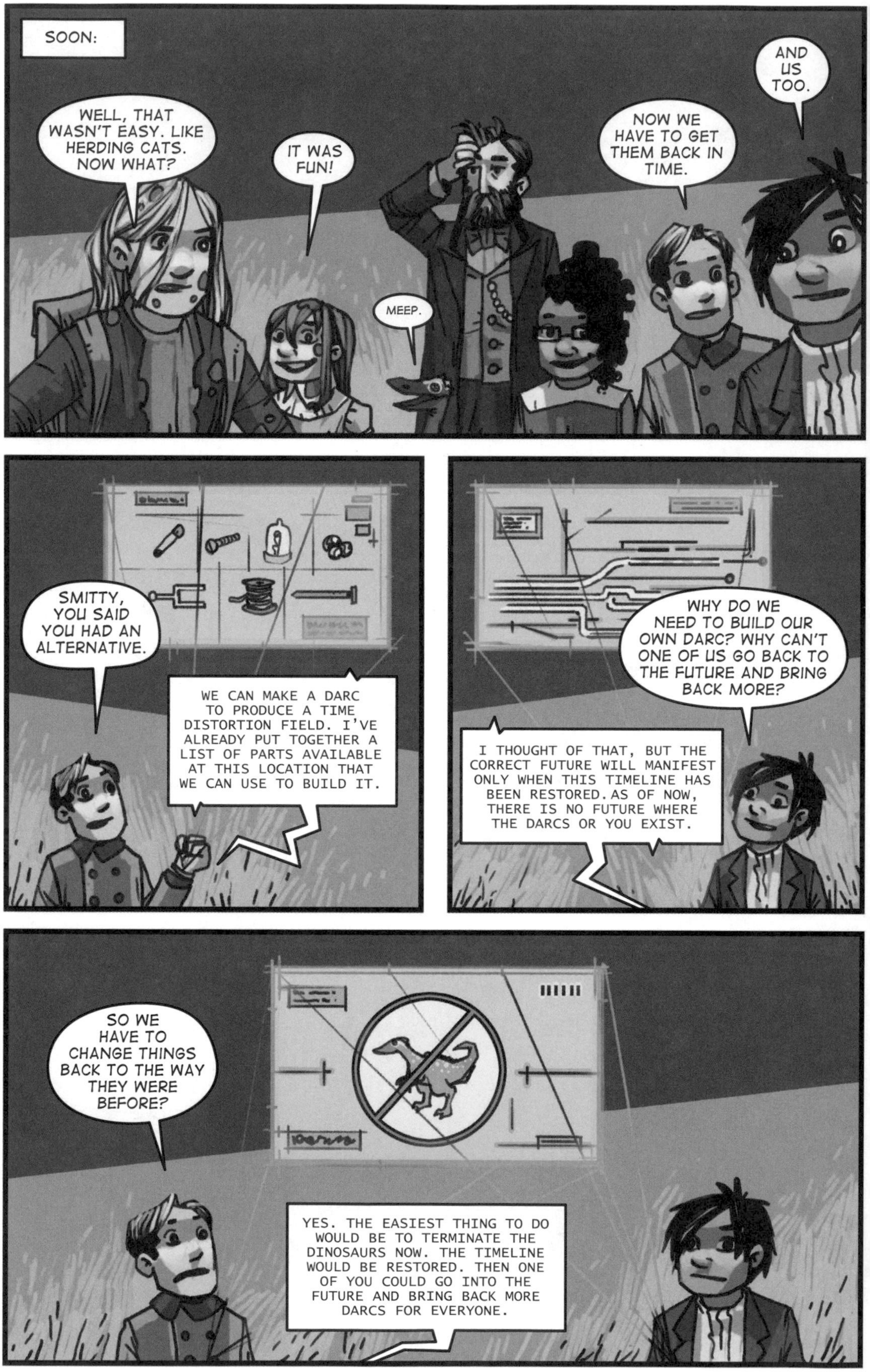
SOON:
WELL, THAT WASN'T EASY. LIKE HERDING CATS. NOW WHAT?
IT WAS FUN!
MEEP.
NOW WE HAVE TO GET THEM BACK IN TIME.
AND US TOO.
SMITTY, YOU SAID YOU HAD AN ALTERNATIVE.
WE CAN MAKE A DARC TO PRODUCE A TIME DISTORTION FIELD. I'VE ALREADY PUT TOGETHER A LIST OF PARTS AVAILABLE AT THIS LOCATION THAT WE CAN USE TO BUILD IT.
WHY DO WE NEED TO BUILD OUR OWN DARC? WHY CAN'T ONE OF US GO BACK TO THE FUTURE AND BRING BACK MORE?
I THOUGHT OF THAT, BUT THE CORRECT FUTURE WILL MANIFEST ONLY WHEN THIS TIMELINE HAS BEEN RESTORED. AS OF NOW, THERE IS NO FUTURE WHERE THE DARCS OR YOU EXIST.
SO WE HAVE TO CHANGE THINGS BACK TO THE WAY THEY WERE BEFORE?
YES. THE EASIEST THING TO DO WOULD BE TO TERMINATE THE DINOSAURS NOW. THE TIMELINE WOULD BE RESTORED. THEN ONE OF YOU COULD GO INTO THE FUTURE AND BRING BACK MORE DARCS FOR EVERYONE.

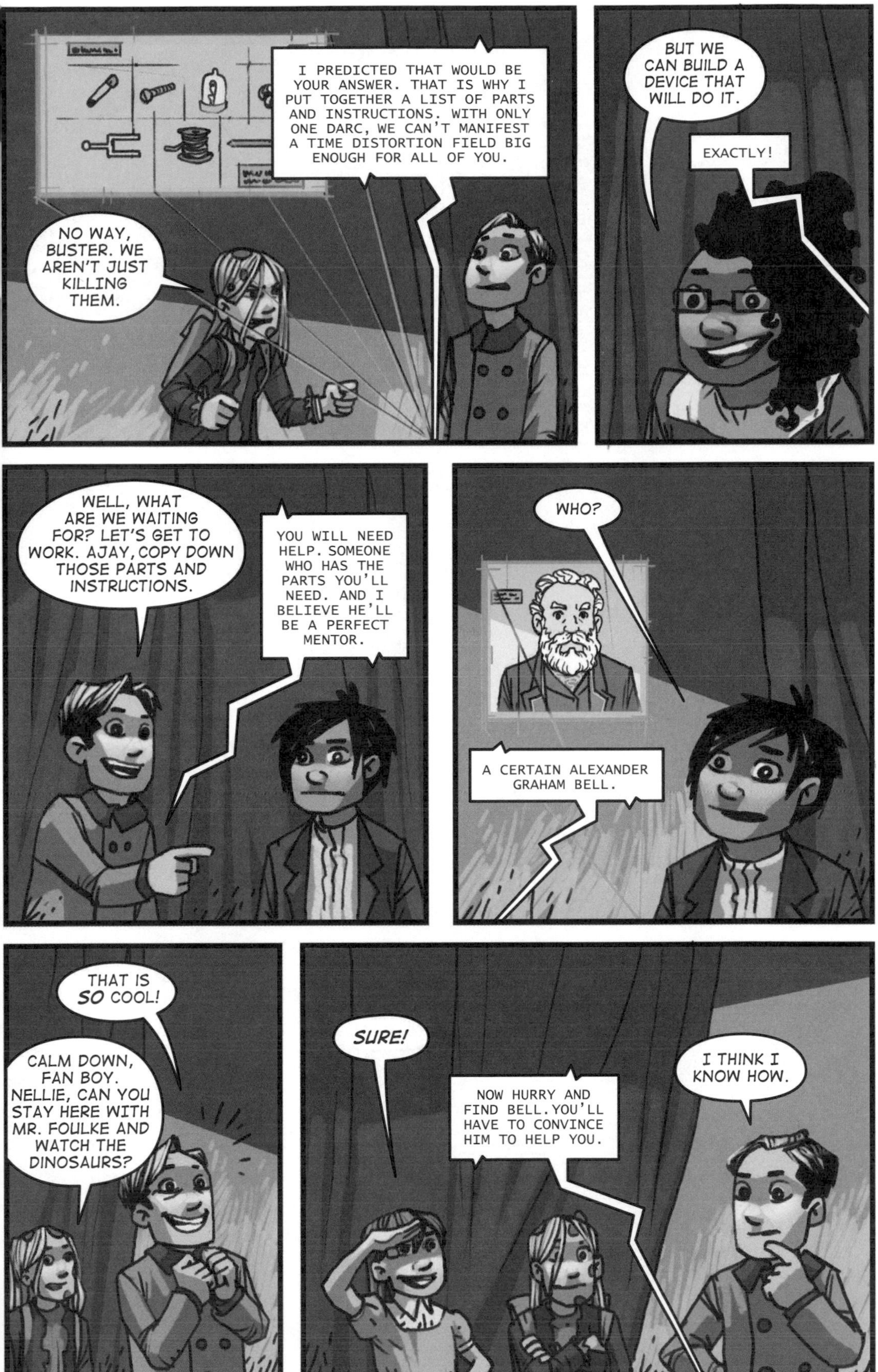
I PREDICTED THAT WOULD BE YOUR ANSWER. THAT IS WHY I PUT TOGETHER A LIST OF PARTS AND INSTRUCTIONS. WITH ONLY ONE DARC, WE CAN'T MANIFEST A TIME DISTORTION FIELD BIG ENOUGH FOR ALL OF YOU.
NO WAY, BUSTER. WE AREN'T JUST KILLING THEM.
BUT WE CAN BUILD A DEVICE THAT WILL DO IT.
EXACTLY!
WELL, WHAT ARE WE WAITING FOR? LET'S GET TO WORK. AJAY, COPY DOWN THOSE PARTS AND INSTRUCTIONS.
YOU WILL NEED HELP. SOMEONE WHO HAS THE PARTS YOU'LL NEED. AND I BELIEVE HE'LL BE A PERFECT MENTOR.
WHO?
A CERTAIN ALEXANDER GRAHAM BELL.
THAT IS SO COOL!
CALM DOWN, FAN BOY. NELLIE, CAN YOU STAY HERE WITH MR. FOULKE AND WATCH THE DINOSAURS?
SURE!
NOW HURRY AND FIND BELL. YOU'LL HAVE TO CONVINCE HIM TO HELP YOU.
I THINK I KNOW HOW.

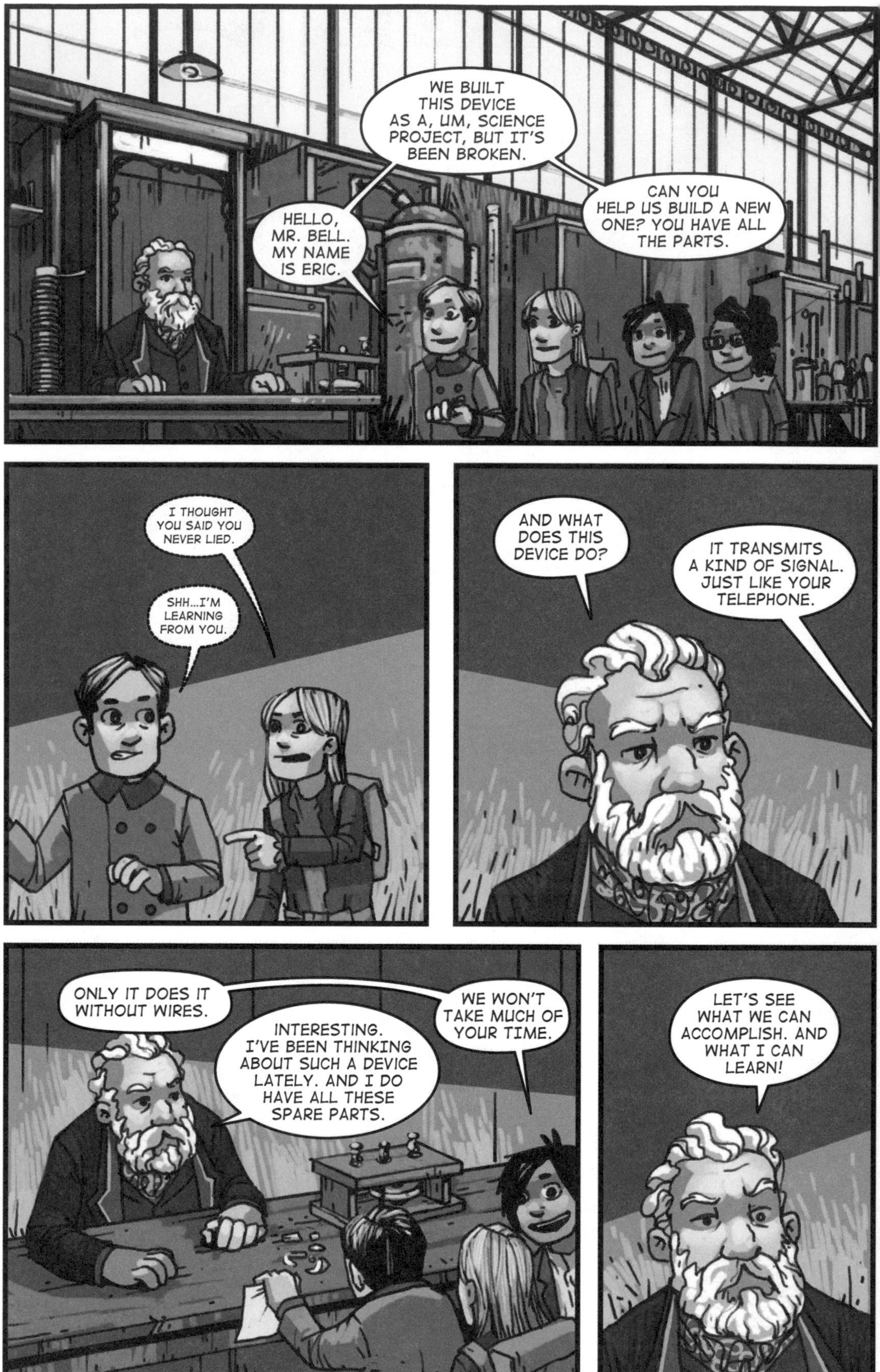
HELLO, MR. BELL. MY NAME IS ERIC.
WE BUILT THIS DEVICE AS A, UM, SCIENCE PROJECT, BUT IT'S BEEN BROKEN.
CAN YOU HELP US BUILD A NEW ONE? YOU HAVE ALL THE PARTS.
I THOUGHT YOU SAID YOU NEVER LIED.
SHH...I'M LEARNING FROM YOU.
AND WHAT DOES THIS DEVICE DO?
IT TRANSMITS A KIND OF SIGNAL. JUST LIKE YOUR TELEPHONE.
ONLY IT DOES IT WITHOUT WIRES.
WE WON'T TAKE MUCH OF YOUR TIME.
INTERESTING. I'VE BEEN THINKING ABOUT SUCH A DEVICE LATELY. AND I DO HAVE ALL THESE SPARE PARTS.
LET'S SEE WHAT WE CAN ACCOMPLISH. AND WHAT I CAN LEARN!

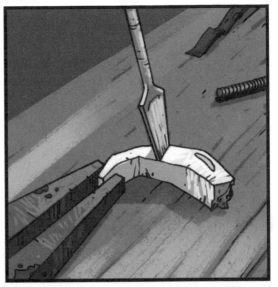

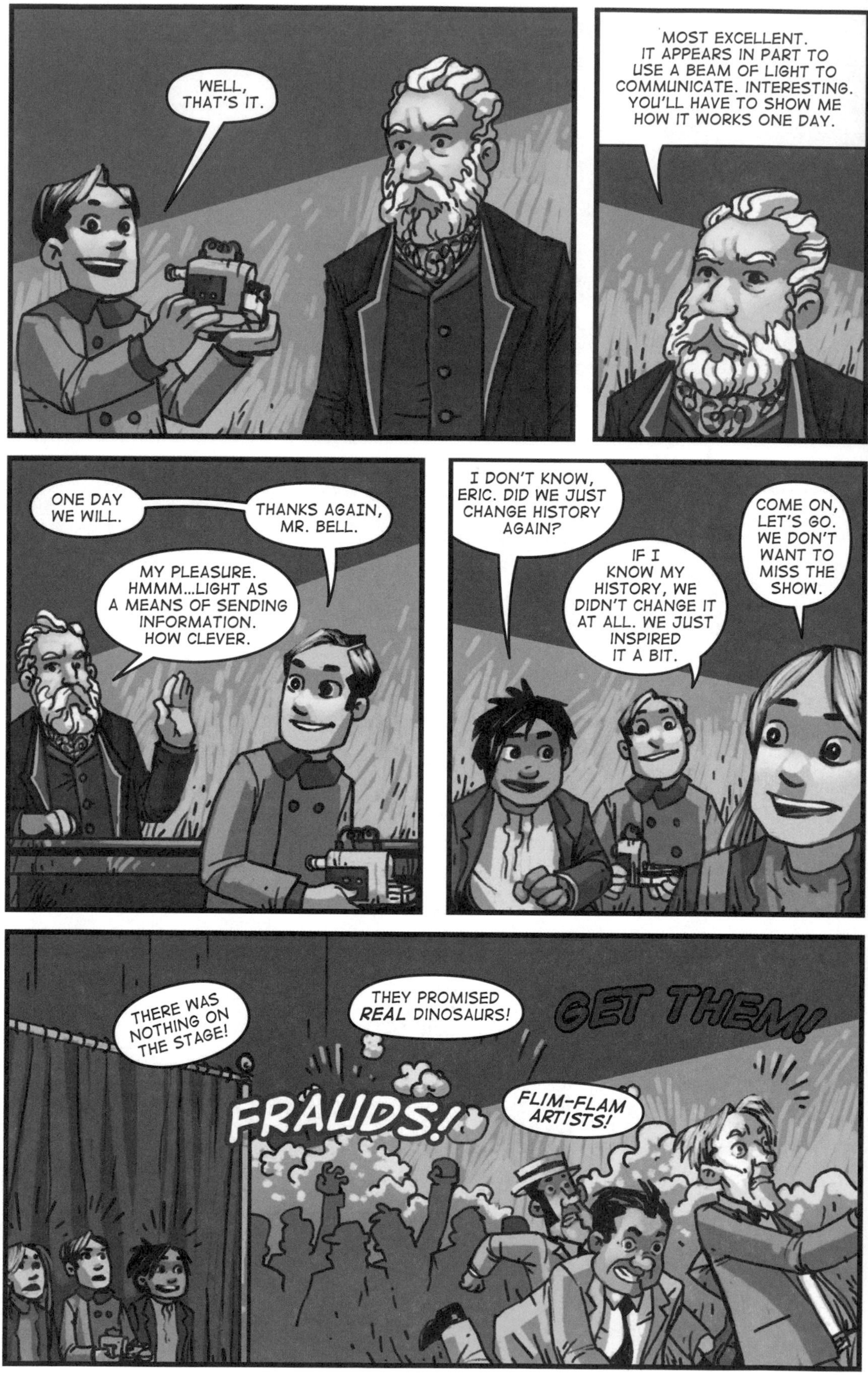
WELL, THAT'S IT.
MOST EXCELLENT. IT APPEARS IN PART TO USE A BEAM OF LIGHT TO COMMUNICATE. INTERESTING. YOU'LL HAVE TO SHOW ME HOW IT WORKS ONE DAY.
ONE DAY WE WILL.
THANKS AGAIN, MR. BELL.
MY PLEASURE. HMMM...LIGHT AS A MEANS OF SENDING INFORMATION. HOW CLEVER.
I DON'T KNOW, ERIC. DID WE JUST CHANGE HISTORY AGAIN?
IF I KNOW MY HISTORY, WE DIDN'T CHANGE IT AT ALL. WE JUST INSPIRED IT A BIT.
COME ON, LET'S GO. WE DON'T WANT TO MISS THE SHOW.
THERE WAS NOTHING ON THE STAGE!
THEY PROMISED *REAL* DINOSAURS!
GET THEM!
FRAUDS!
FLIM-FLAM ARTISTS!

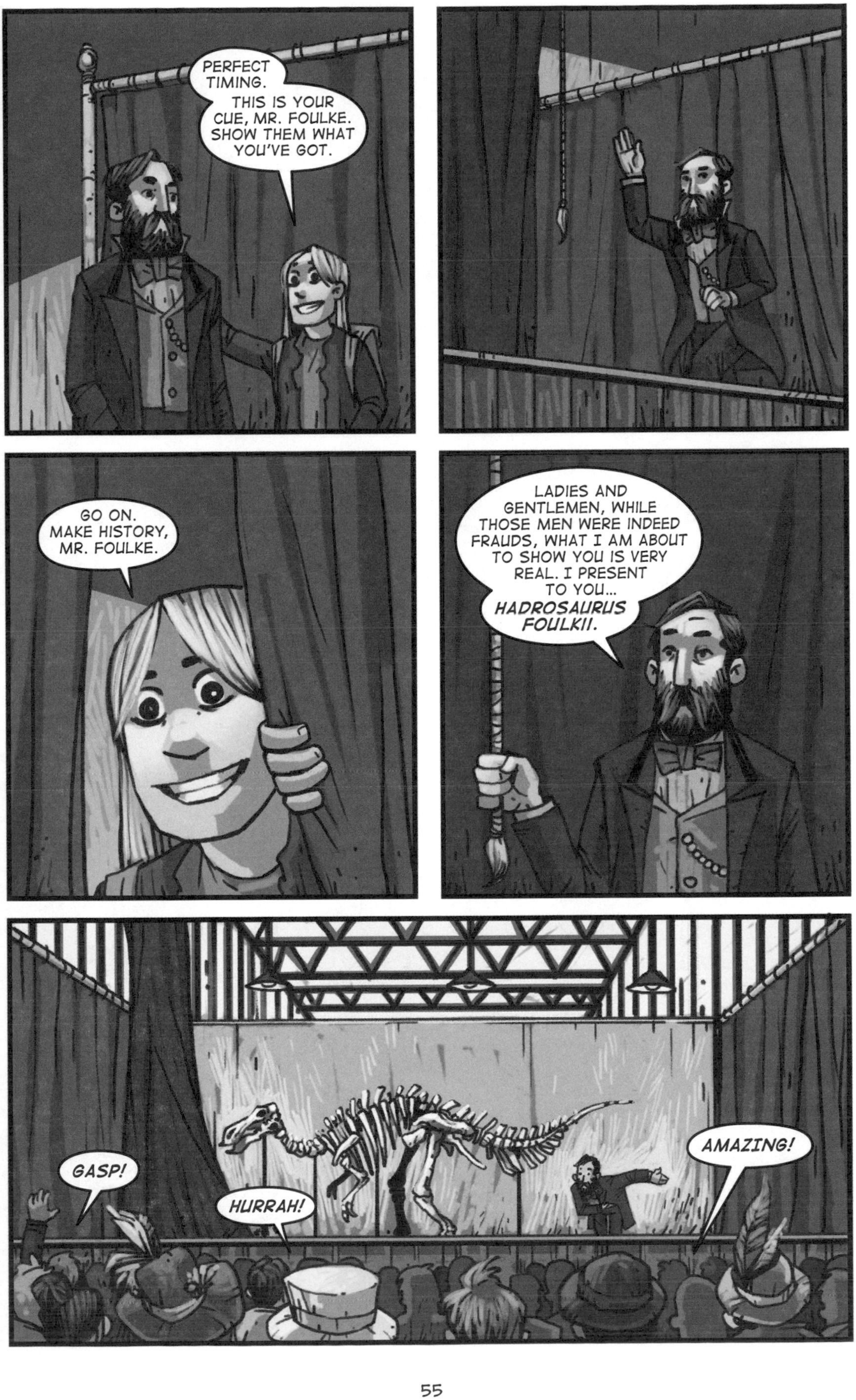
PERFECT TIMING.
THIS IS YOUR CUE, MR. FOULKE. SHOW THEM WHAT YOU'VE GOT.
GO ON. MAKE HISTORY, MR. FOULKE.
LADIES AND GENTLEMEN, WHILE THOSE MEN WERE INDEED FRAUDS, WHAT I AM ABOUT TO SHOW YOU IS VERY REAL. I PRESENT TO YOU... *HADROSAURUS FOULKII.*
GASP!
HURRAH!
AMAZING!

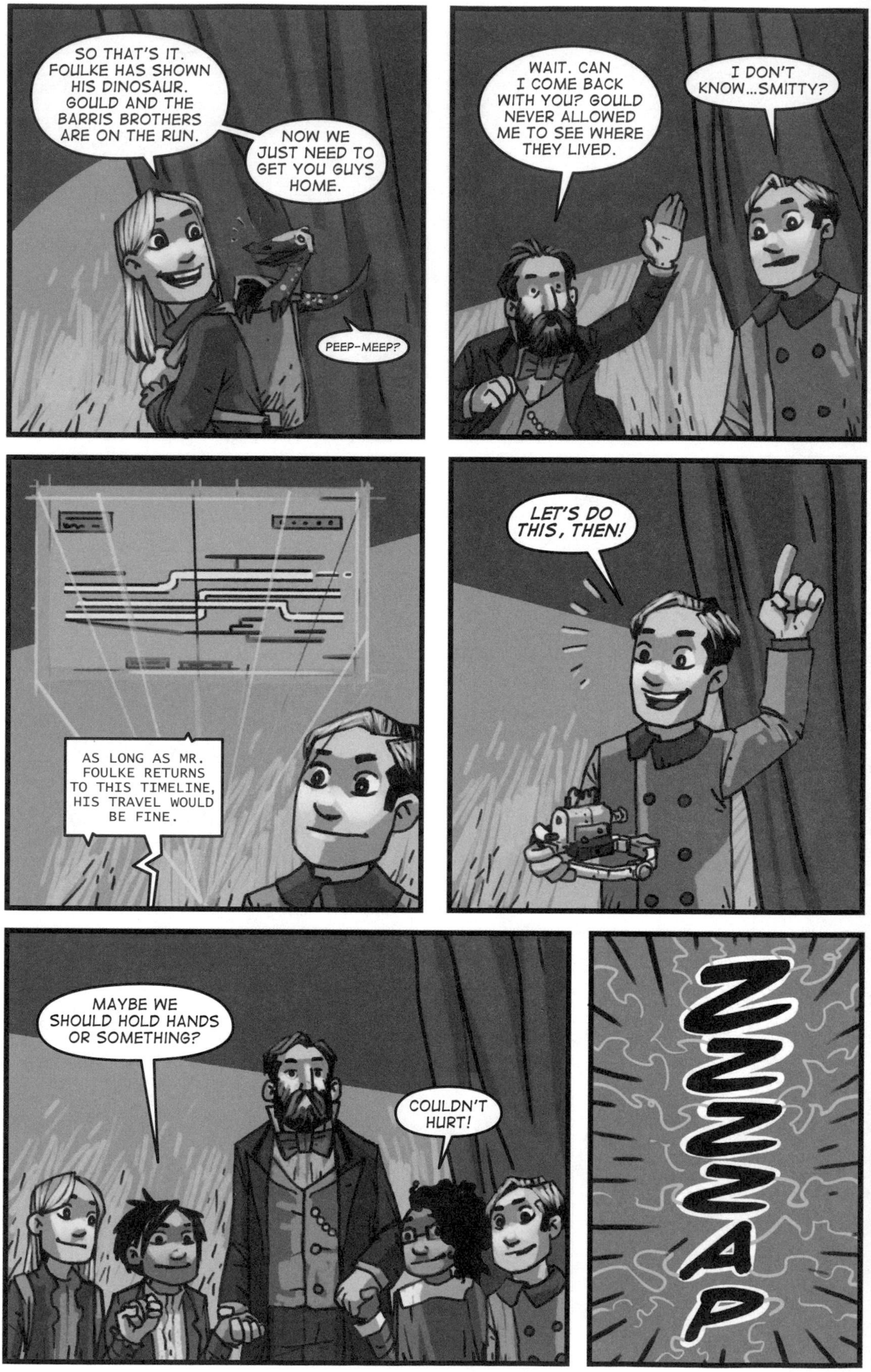
SO THAT'S IT. FOULKE HAS SHOWN HIS DINOSAUR. GOULD AND THE BARRIS BROTHERS ARE ON THE RUN.
NOW WE JUST NEED TO GET YOU GUYS HOME.
PEEP-MEEP?
WAIT. CAN I COME BACK WITH YOU? GOULD NEVER ALLOWED ME TO SEE WHERE THEY LIVED.
I DON'T KNOW...SMITTY?
AS LONG AS MR. FOULKE RETURNS TO THIS TIMELINE, HIS TRAVEL WOULD BE FINE.
LET'S DO THIS, THEN!
MAYBE WE SHOULD HOLD HANDS OR SOMETHING?
COULDN'T HURT!
ZZZZZAP

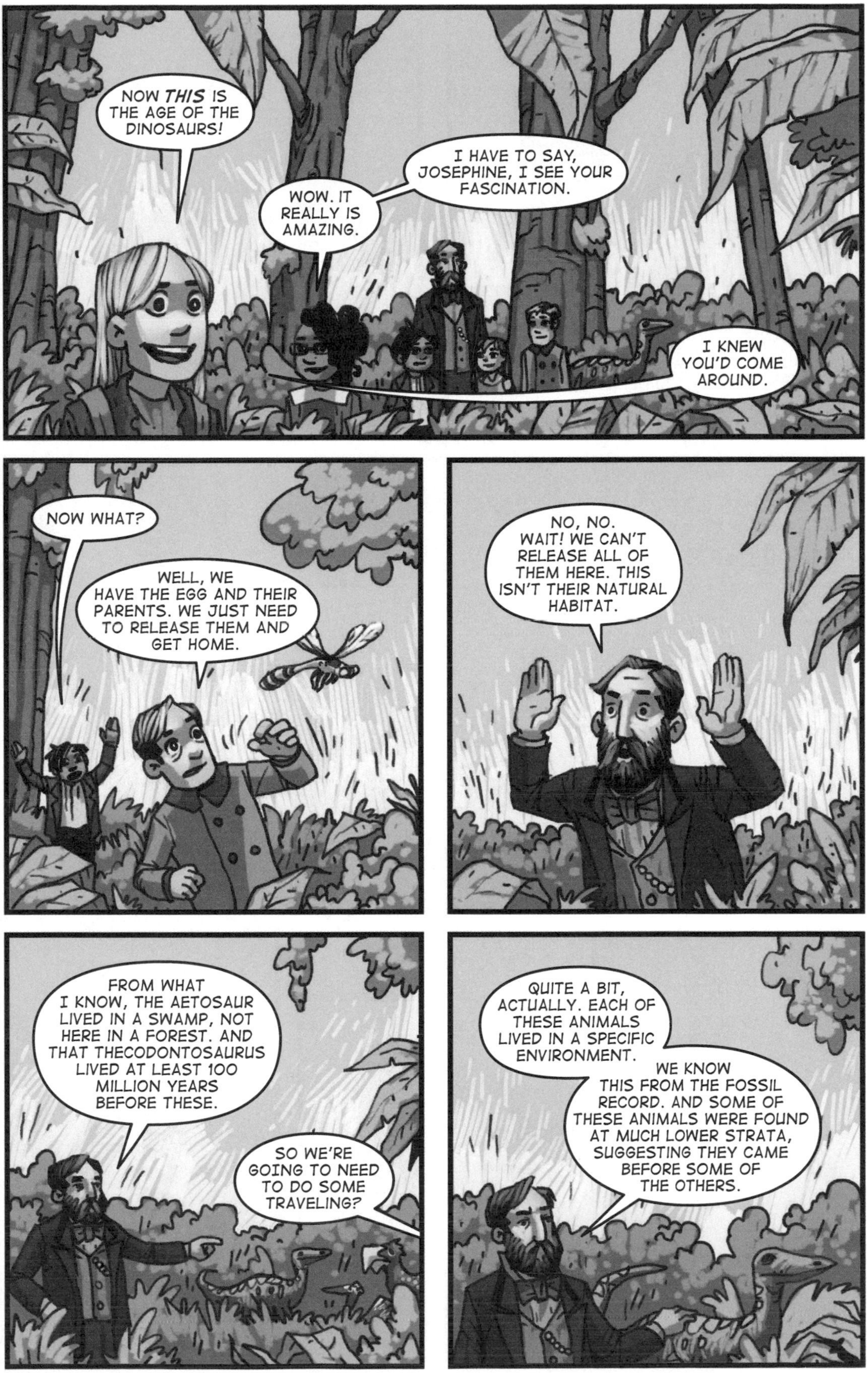

NOW *THIS* IS THE AGE OF THE DINOSAURS!
WOW. IT REALLY IS AMAZING.
I HAVE TO SAY, JOSEPHINE, I SEE YOUR FASCINATION.
I KNEW YOU'D COME AROUND.
NOW WHAT?
WELL, WE HAVE THE EGG AND THEIR PARENTS. WE JUST NEED TO RELEASE THEM AND GET HOME.
NO, NO. WAIT! WE CAN'T RELEASE ALL OF THEM HERE. THIS ISN'T THEIR NATURAL HABITAT.
FROM WHAT I KNOW, THE AETOSAUR LIVED IN A SWAMP, NOT HERE IN A FOREST. AND THAT THECODONTOSAURUS LIVED AT LEAST 100 MILLION YEARS BEFORE THESE.
SO WE'RE GOING TO NEED TO DO SOME TRAVELING?
QUITE A BIT, ACTUALLY. EACH OF THESE ANIMALS LIVED IN A SPECIFIC ENVIRONMENT.
WE KNOW THIS FROM THE FOSSIL RECORD. AND SOME OF THESE ANIMALS WERE FOUND AT MUCH LOWER STRATA, SUGGESTING THEY CAME BEFORE SOME OF THE OTHERS.

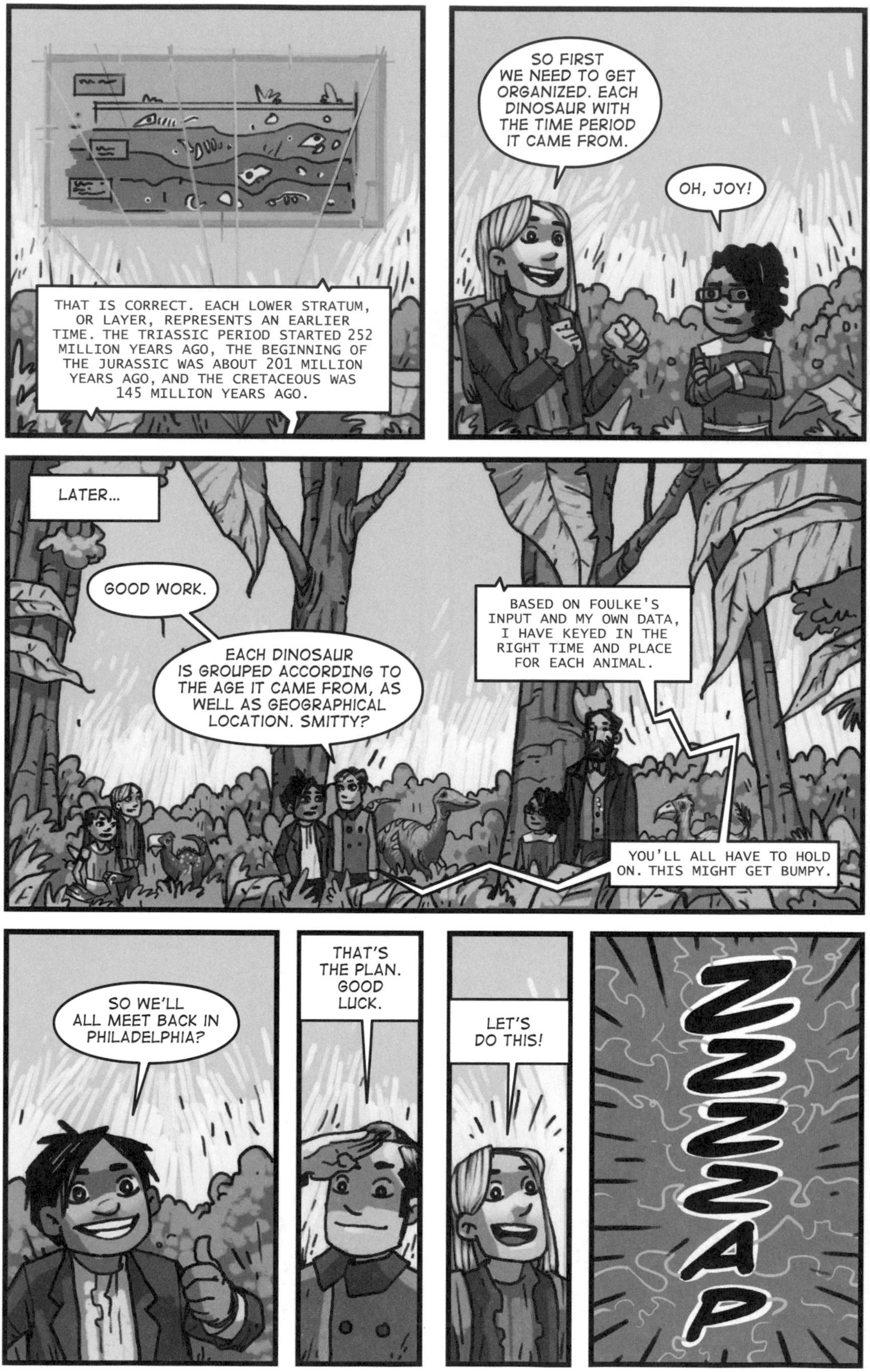
THAT IS CORRECT. EACH LOWER STRATUM, OR LAYER, REPRESENTS AN EARLIER TIME. THE TRIASSIC PERIOD STARTED 252 MILLION YEARS AGO, THE BEGINNING OF THE JURASSIC WAS ABOUT 201 MILLION YEARS AGO, AND THE CRETACEOUS WAS 145 MILLION YEARS AGO.
SO FIRST WE NEED TO GET ORGANIZED. EACH DINOSAUR WITH THE TIME PERIOD IT CAME FROM.
OH, JOY!
LATER...
GOOD WORK.
EACH DINOSAUR IS GROUPED ACCORDING TO THE AGE IT CAME FROM, AS WELL AS GEOGRAPHICAL LOCATION. SMITTY?
BASED ON FOULKE'S INPUT AND MY OWN DATA, I HAVE KEYED IN THE RIGHT TIME AND PLACE FOR EACH ANIMAL.
YOU'LL ALL HAVE TO HOLD ON. THIS MIGHT GET BUMPY.
SO WE'LL ALL MEET BACK IN PHILADELPHIA?
THAT'S THE PLAN. GOOD LUCK.
LET'S DO THIS!
ZZZZAP

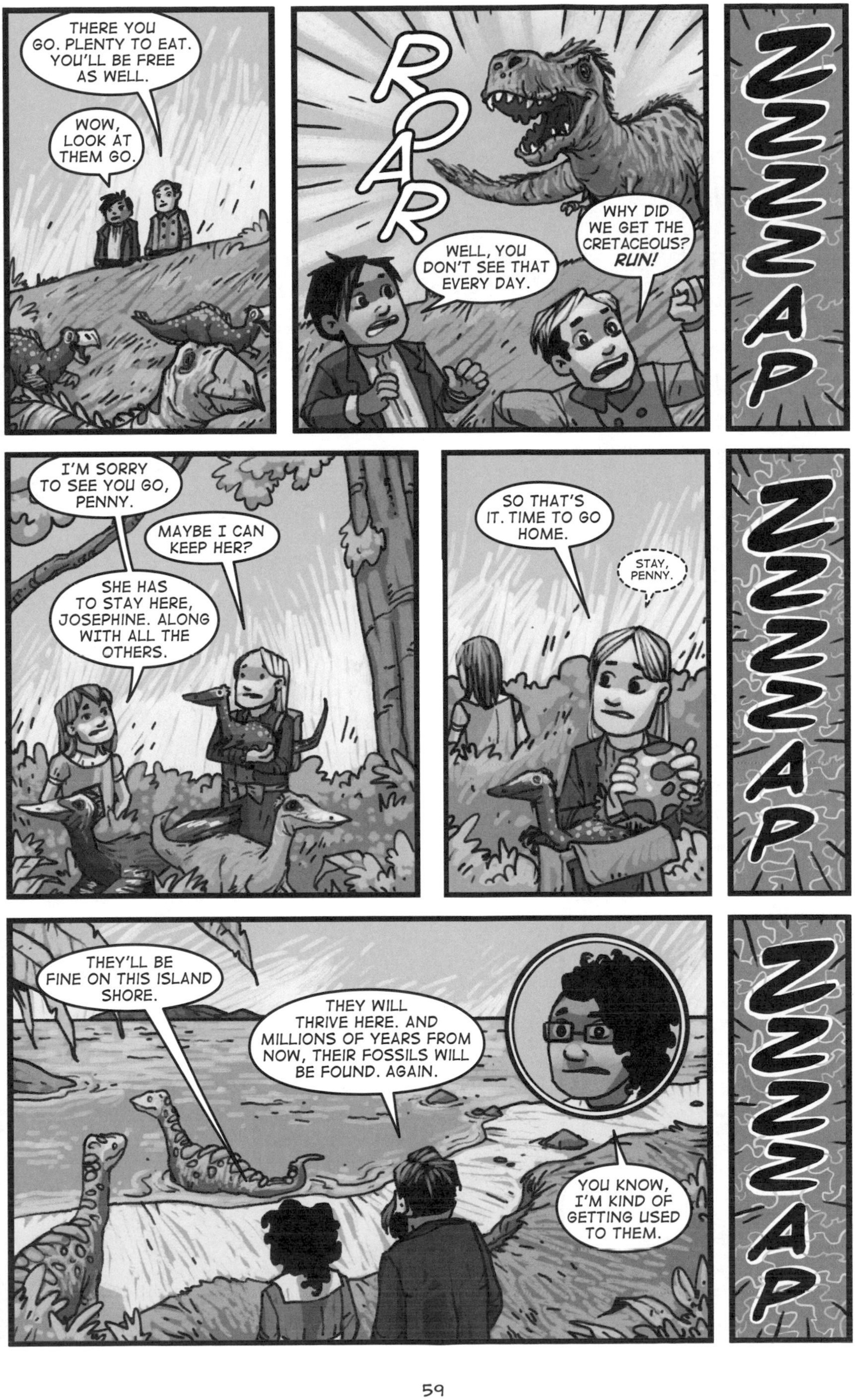

THERE YOU GO. PLENTY TO EAT. YOU'LL BE FREE AS WELL.
WOW, LOOK AT THEM GO.
ROAR
WELL, YOU DON'T SEE THAT EVERY DAY.
WHY DID WE GET THE CRETACEOUS? *RUN!*
ZZZZAP
I'M SORRY TO SEE YOU GO, PENNY.
MAYBE I CAN KEEP HER?
SHE HAS TO STAY HERE, JOSEPHINE. ALONG WITH ALL THE OTHERS.
SO THAT'S IT. TIME TO GO HOME.
STAY, PENNY.
ZZZZAP
THEY'LL BE FINE ON THIS ISLAND SHORE.
THEY WILL THRIVE HERE. AND MILLIONS OF YEARS FROM NOW, THEIR FOSSILS WILL BE FOUND. AGAIN.
YOU KNOW, I'M KIND OF GETTING USED TO THEM.
ZZZZAP

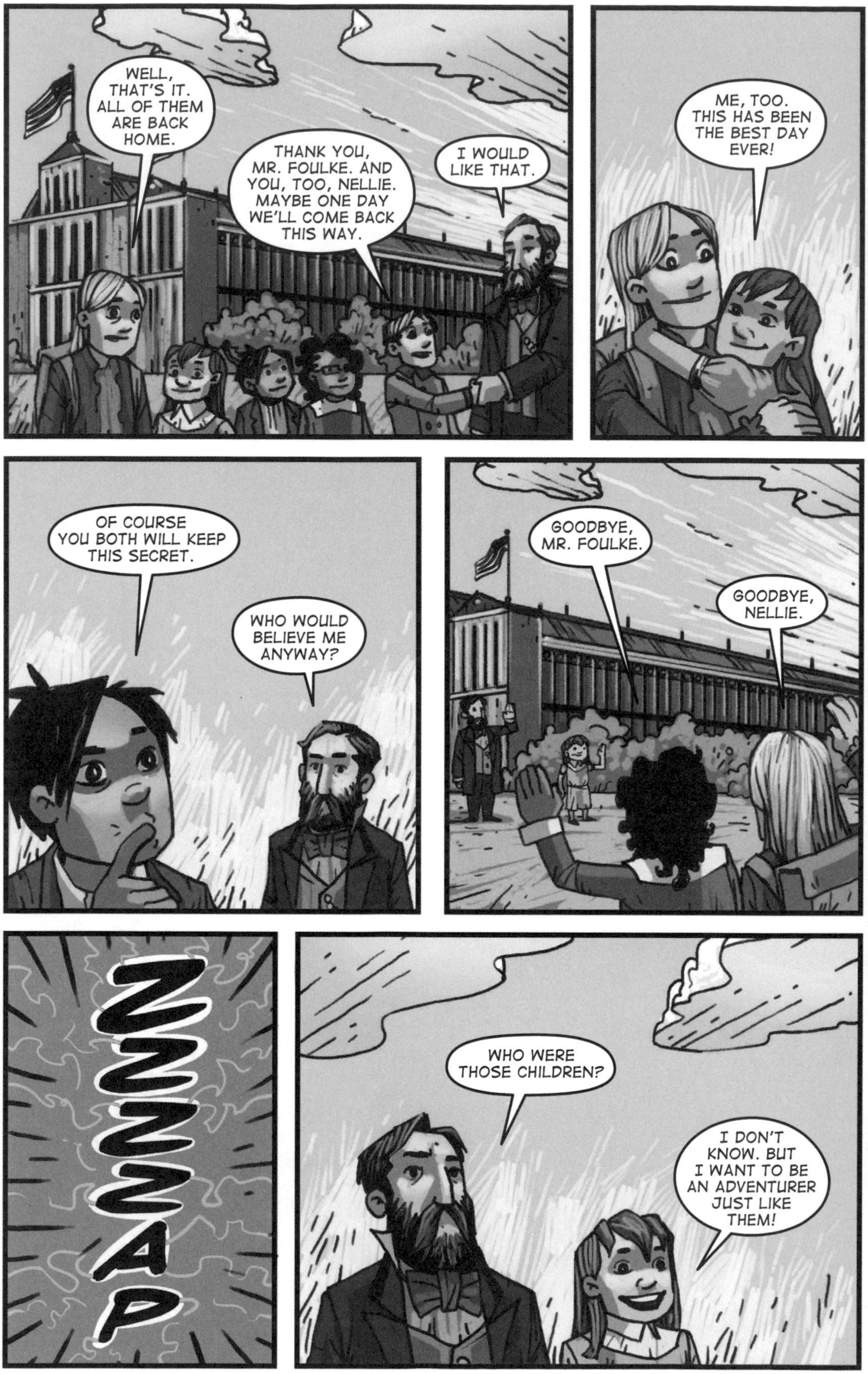
WELL, THAT'S IT. ALL OF THEM ARE BACK HOME.
THANK YOU, MR. FOULKE. AND YOU, TOO, NELLIE. MAYBE ONE DAY WE'LL COME BACK THIS WAY.
I WOULD LIKE THAT.
ME, TOO. THIS HAS BEEN THE BEST DAY EVER!
OF COURSE YOU BOTH WILL KEEP THIS SECRET.
WHO WOULD BELIEVE ME ANYWAY?
GOODBYE, MR. FOULKE.
GOODBYE, NELLIE.
ZZZZAP
WHO WERE THOSE CHILDREN?
I DON'T KNOW. BUT I WANT TO BE AN ADVENTURER JUST LIKE THEM!

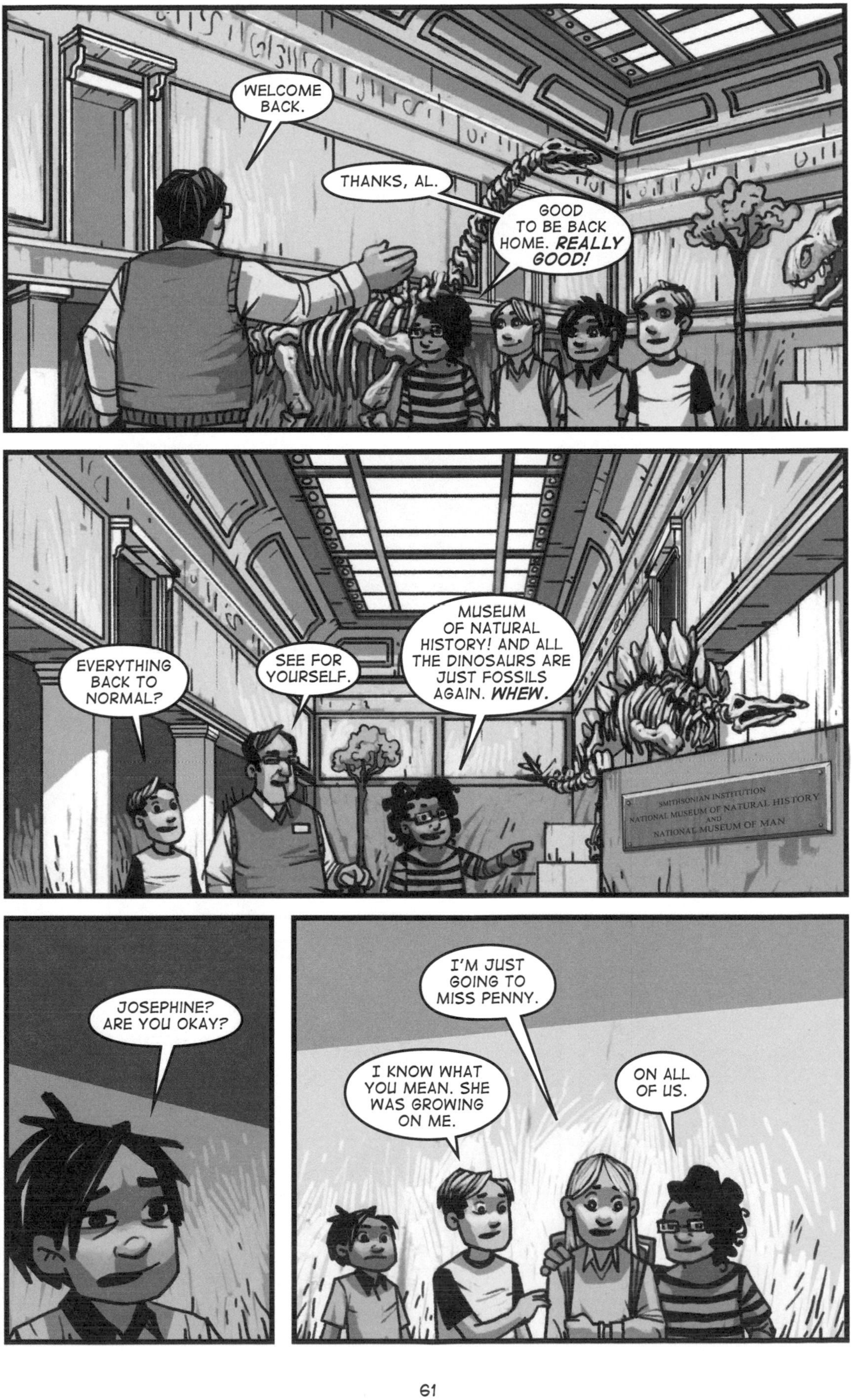
WELCOME BACK.
THANKS, AL.
GOOD TO BE BACK HOME. REALLY GOOD!
EVERYTHING BACK TO NORMAL?
SEE FOR YOURSELF.
MUSEUM OF NATURAL HISTORY! AND ALL THE DINOSAURS ARE JUST FOSSILS AGAIN. WHEW.
SMITHSONIAN INSTITUTION
NATIONAL MUSEUM OF NATURAL HISTORY
AND
NATIONAL MUSEUM OF MAN
JOSEPHINE? ARE YOU OKAY?
I'M JUST GOING TO MISS PENNY.
I KNOW WHAT YOU MEAN. SHE WAS GROWING ON ME.
ON ALL OF US.

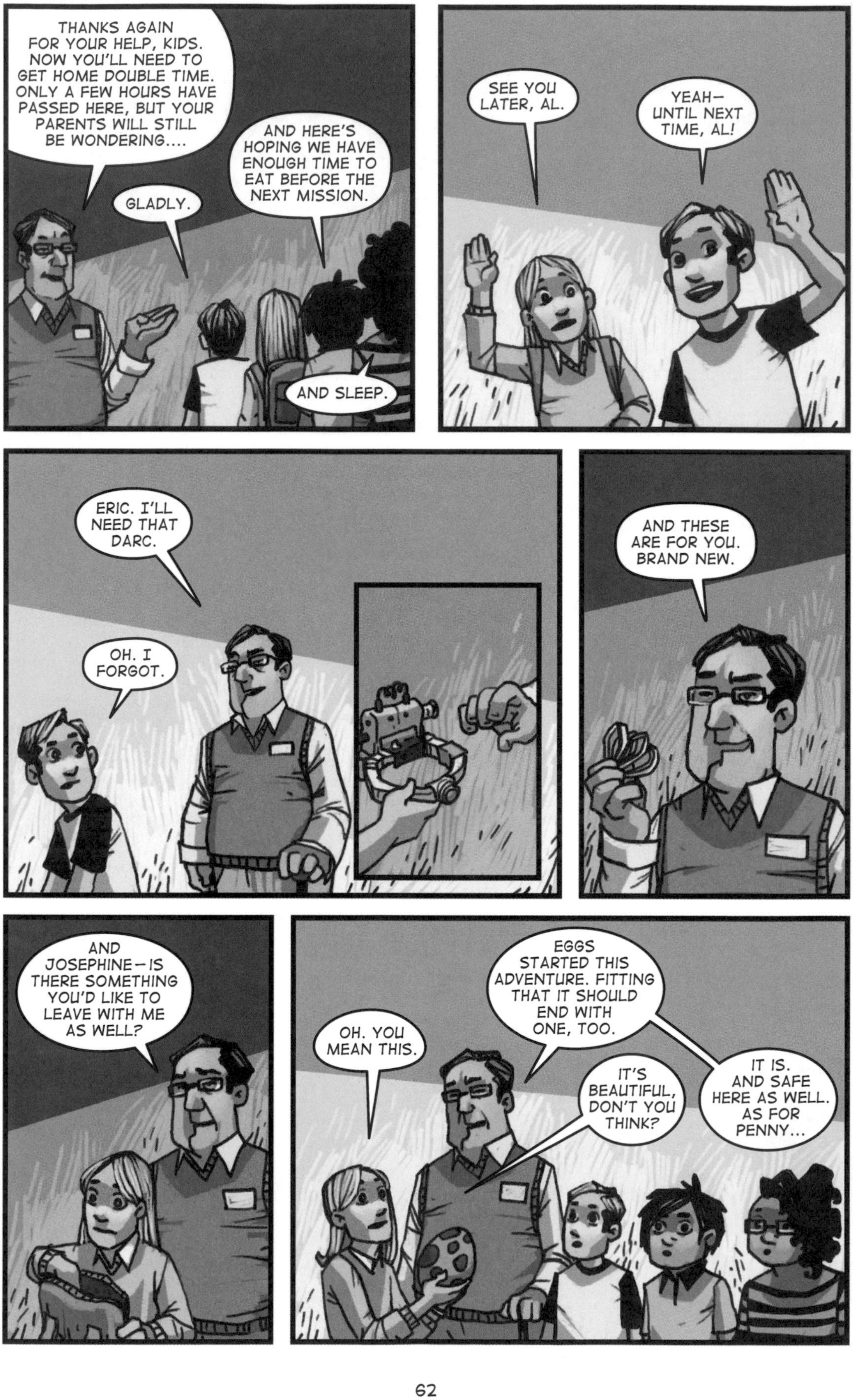
THANKS AGAIN FOR YOUR HELP, KIDS. NOW YOU'LL NEED TO GET HOME DOUBLE TIME. ONLY A FEW HOURS HAVE PASSED HERE, BUT YOUR PARENTS WILL STILL BE WONDERING....
GLADLY.
AND HERE'S HOPING WE HAVE ENOUGH TIME TO EAT BEFORE THE NEXT MISSION.
AND SLEEP.
SEE YOU LATER, AL.
YEAH—UNTIL NEXT TIME, AL!
ERIC. I'LL NEED THAT DARC.
OH. I FORGOT.
AND THESE ARE FOR YOU. BRAND NEW.
AND JOSEPHINE—IS THERE SOMETHING YOU'D LIKE TO LEAVE WITH ME AS WELL?
OH. YOU MEAN THIS.
EGGS STARTED THIS ADVENTURE. FITTING THAT IT SHOULD END WITH ONE, TOO.
IT'S BEAUTIFUL, DON'T YOU THINK?
IT IS. AND SAFE HERE AS WELL. AS FOR PENNY...

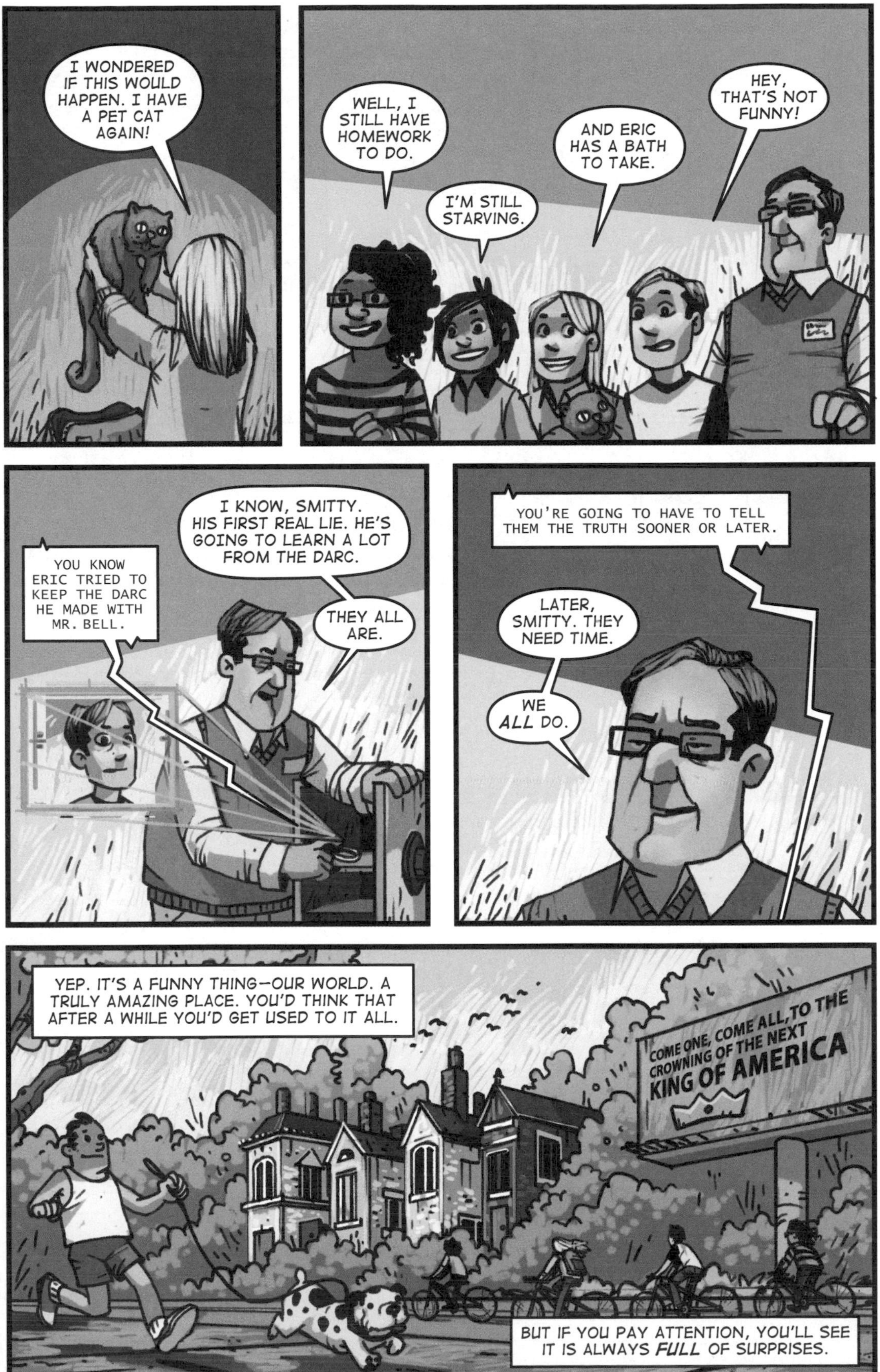
I WONDERED IF THIS WOULD HAPPEN. I HAVE A PET CAT AGAIN!
WELL, I STILL HAVE HOMEWORK TO DO.
I'M STILL STARVING.
AND ERIC HAS A BATH TO TAKE.
HEY, THAT'S NOT FUNNY!
YOU KNOW ERIC TRIED TO KEEP THE DARC HE MADE WITH MR. BELL.
I KNOW, SMITTY. HIS FIRST REAL LIE. HE'S GOING TO LEARN A LOT FROM THE DARC.
THEY ALL ARE.
YOU'RE GOING TO HAVE TO TELL THEM THE TRUTH SOONER OR LATER.
LATER, SMITTY. THEY NEED TIME.
WE *ALL* DO.
YEP. IT'S A FUNNY THING—OUR WORLD. A TRULY AMAZING PLACE. YOU'D THINK THAT AFTER A WHILE YOU'D GET USED TO IT ALL.
COME ONE, COME ALL, TO THE CROWNING OF THE NEXT KING OF AMERICA
BUT IF YOU PAY ATTENTION, YOU'LL SEE IT IS ALWAYS *FULL* OF SURPRISES.

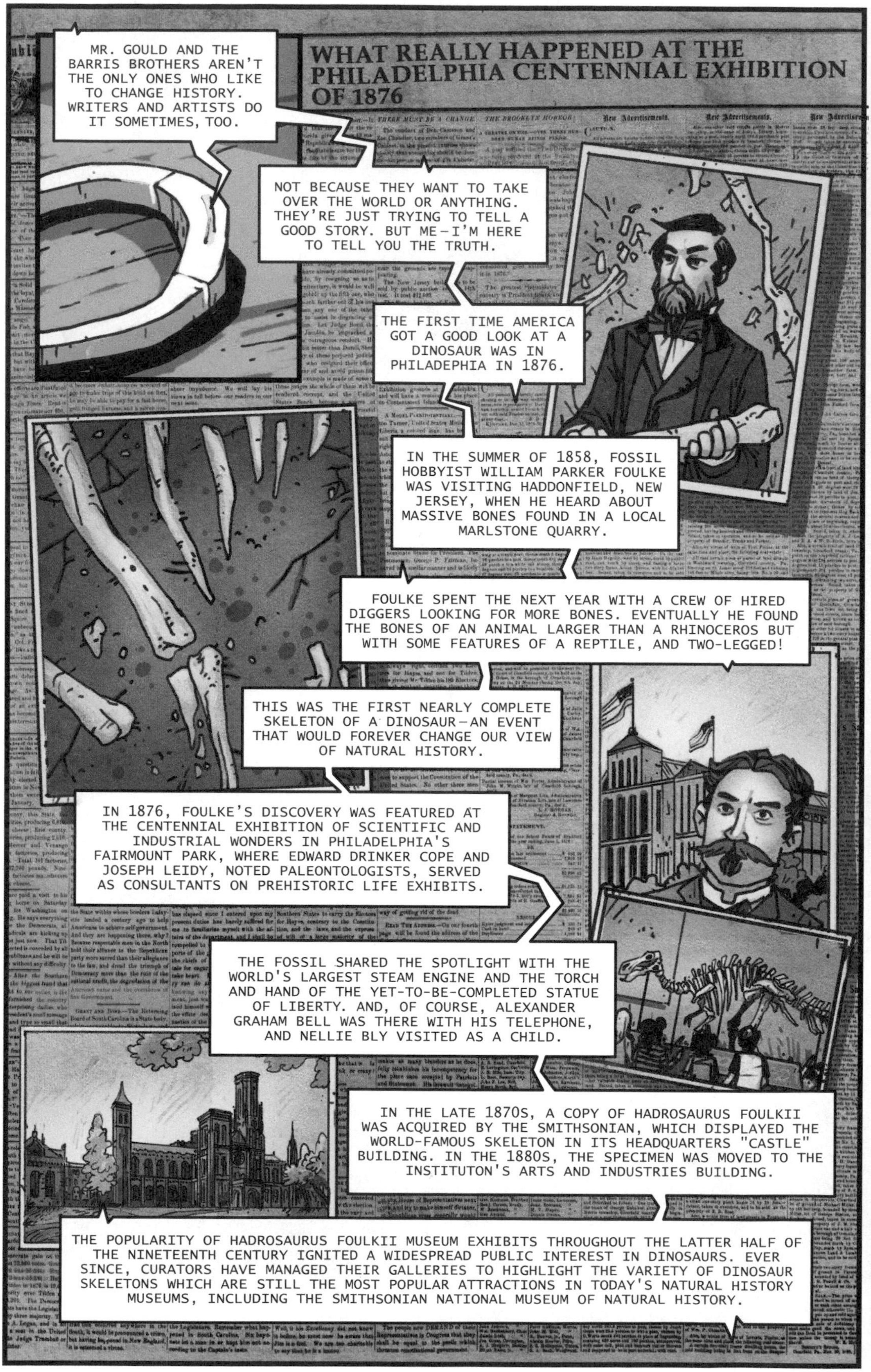
WHAT REALLY HAPPENED AT THE PHILADELPHIA CENTENNIAL EXHIBITION OF 1876
MR. GOULD AND THE BARRIS BROTHERS AREN'T THE ONLY ONES WHO LIKE TO CHANGE HISTORY. WRITERS AND ARTISTS DO IT SOMETIMES, TOO.
NOT BECAUSE THEY WANT TO TAKE OVER THE WORLD OR ANYTHING. THEY'RE JUST TRYING TO TELL A GOOD STORY. BUT ME—I'M HERE TO TELL YOU THE TRUTH.
THE FIRST TIME AMERICA GOT A GOOD LOOK AT A DINOSAUR WAS IN PHILADEPHIA IN 1876.
IN THE SUMMER OF 1858, FOSSIL HOBBYIST WILLIAM PARKER FOULKE WAS VISITING HADDONFIELD, NEW JERSEY, WHEN HE HEARD ABOUT MASSIVE BONES FOUND IN A LOCAL MARLSTONE QUARRY.
FOULKE SPENT THE NEXT YEAR WITH A CREW OF HIRED DIGGERS LOOKING FOR MORE BONES. EVENTUALLY HE FOUND THE BONES OF AN ANIMAL LARGER THAN A RHINOCEROS BUT WITH SOME FEATURES OF A REPTILE, AND TWO-LEGGED!
THIS WAS THE FIRST NEARLY COMPLETE SKELETON OF A DINOSAUR—AN EVENT THAT WOULD FOREVER CHANGE OUR VIEW OF NATURAL HISTORY.
IN 1876, FOULKE'S DISCOVERY WAS FEATURED AT THE CENTENNIAL EXHIBITION OF SCIENTIFIC AND INDUSTRIAL WONDERS IN PHILADELPHIA'S FAIRMOUNT PARK, WHERE EDWARD DRINKER COPE AND JOSEPH LEIDY, NOTED PALEONTOLOGISTS, SERVED AS CONSULTANTS ON PREHISTORIC LIFE EXHIBITS.
THE FOSSIL SHARED THE SPOTLIGHT WITH THE WORLD'S LARGEST STEAM ENGINE AND THE TORCH AND HAND OF THE YET-TO-BE-COMPLETED STATUE OF LIBERTY. AND, OF COURSE, ALEXANDER GRAHAM BELL WAS THERE WITH HIS TELEPHONE, AND NELLIE BLY VISITED AS A CHILD.
IN THE LATE 1870S, A COPY OF HADROSAURUS FOULKII WAS ACQUIRED BY THE SMITHSONIAN, WHICH DISPLAYED THE WORLD-FAMOUS SKELETON IN ITS HEADQUARTERS "CASTLE" BUILDING. IN THE 1880S, THE SPECIMEN WAS MOVED TO THE INSTITUTON'S ARTS AND INDUSTRIES BUILDING.
THE POPULARITY OF HADROSAURUS FOULKII MUSEUM EXHIBITS THROUGHOUT THE LATTER HALF OF THE NINETEENTH CENTURY IGNITED A WIDESPREAD PUBLIC INTEREST IN DINOSAURS. EVER SINCE, CURATORS HAVE MANAGED THEIR GALLERIES TO HIGHLIGHT THE VARIETY OF DINOSAUR SKELETONS WHICH ARE STILL THE MOST POPULAR ATTRACTIONS IN TODAY'S NATURAL HISTORY MUSEUMS, INCLUDING THE SMITHSONIAN NATIONAL MUSEUM OF NATURAL HISTORY.